THE
SIMPLE
LIFE

GUIDE TO DECLUTTERING YOUR LIFE

Other Books by Gary Collins

The Simple Life Guide To RV Living:
The Road to Freedom and the Mobile Lifestyle Revolution

The Simple Life Guide To Optimal Health:
How to Get Healthy, Lose Weight, Reverse Disease and Feel Better Than Ever

The Beginners Guide To Living Off The Grid:
The DIY Workbook for Living the Life You Want

Living Off The Grid: *What to Expect While Living the Life of Ultimate Freedom and Tranquility*

Going Off The Grid: *The How-To Book of Simple Living and Happiness*

THE SIMPLE LIFE

GUIDE TO DECLUTTERING YOUR LIFE

The How-To Book of Doing More with Less
and Focusing on the Things That Matter

GARY COLLINS, MS

The Simple Life Series (Book 3)

The Simple Life Guide To Decluttering Your Life: The How-To Book of Doing More with Less and Focusing on the Things That Matter

First Edition

Printed in the United States of America

Copyright ©2019

Published by Second Nature Publishing, Albuquerque, NM 87109

Cover and interior design by Laurie Griffin | www.LaurieGriffin.com

DISCLAIMER OF WARRANTY

ISBN 978-1-57067-384-9

FSC
www.fsc.org
MIX
Paper from
responsible sources
FSC® C005010

Get Your Free Goodies and Be a Part of My Special Community!

Building a solid relationship with my readers is incredibly important to me. It's one of the rewards of being a writer. From time to time, I send out my newsletter (never spammy, I promise) to keep you up-to-date with special offers and information about anything new I may be doing. I've moved away from using social media in the pursuit of a simpler life, so if you want to be part of the "in crowd," my newsletter and blog are the place to be.

If that's not enough enticement, when you sign up for my newsletter I'll send you some spectacular free stuff!

- Chapter from *The Simple Life Guide To Optimal Health* about the dirty little secrets of the supplement industry, and how to make informed purchasing decisions

- 10% off and free shipping on your first order at www.thesimplelifenow.com

You can get all the goodies above by signing up for my mailing list at: www.thesimplelifenow.com/declutter.

TABLE OF CONTENTS

INTRODUCTION

What Is This Book About?

I'll start first with what this book is *not* about—it's not about how to organize your closets, or tips and tricks on keeping your house clean. There are numerous books on those topics, and I feel most of them are missing the elephants in the room: our life choices that are doing us harm. Don't get me wrong, organization will be discussed, but primarily in the area of organizing your life. Your home is only a small piece of the puzzle, as there are many other things in your life you must confront and change to begin living the life **YOU** want.

Decluttering has many different meanings, depending on who you talk to and what subject you're discussing. For me, decluttering is about removing the unnecessary internal and external stressors in my life in order to live the life I want. For others, it could range from living in the woods in a house off the grid, to minimizing possessions and downsizing one's life. No matter where you live or the type of lifestyle you're living, I think everyone could use at least a little bit of decluttering in their life.

It's no secret today that we're bombarded by outside stressors that are unfamiliar to earlier generations of humans, and we're struggling to deal with them. Not a moment goes by where we're not marketed to and told that purchasing items promises happiness. We're taught from the time we enter this world that we must be the ultimate consumer—buy, buy, buy in an attempt to fill the void of our unhappiness with shiny objects. The result: We're witnessing an epidemic of obesity, depression, anxiety, and overall dissatisfaction with our lives today. So we know that having more items does not equal happiness.

It's estimated that close to $200 billion dollars was spent in the year 2018 in the United States on marketing. We've become so conditioned to incessant marketing, for products that are supposed cure our blues, that we don't even realize when it slaps us directly in the face. According to the Centers for Disease Control (CDC), in 2016 $9.5 billion was spent on marketing cigarettes and smokeless tobacco in the United States. This amount translates to about $26 million each day, or more than $1 million every hour. I find it pretty amazing that that much money is spent in order to get us addicted and slowly kill us. But trust me, the tobacco industry wouldn't be spending that kind of money if it didn't make them a fat profit at the expense of our health and finances. Below is the result and an example of the damage our consumer-based society causes. Self-inflicted, I may add.

Smoking-related illnesses in the United States cost more than $300 billion each year, including:

• Nearly $170 billion for direct medical care for adults

- More than $156 billion in lost productivity, including $5.6 billion in lost productivity due to secondhand smoke exposure

I use the above as an example of how successful, targeted marketing can work, and how it can influence us to do things that are actually harmful to us. Did you know pharmaceutical companies aren't allowed to advertise on television in Europe? The reason is that the governments in Europe have realized how influential these advertisements can be. Not in the good old United States of America—we're blitzed with constant pharmaceutical ads telling us they have the cure for whatever's ailing us, even when we didn't know it was ailing us to begin with!

As a matter of fact, I know this firsthand as I used follow the shopaholic mantra just like everyone else. It took me four decades to figure it out, but I finally made the change and decided to live the life I want. I'll share my story here, along with what I've learned while on my journey to a life of ultimate simplicity and happiness.

During my years consulting with clients about their health, I learned that many were having daily struggles outside of their health issues. As with all of my books, my goal is to motivate, educate, and help you put into action the things that will make your life easier and hopefully more enjoyable.

With any changes you make in life, there's usually some pain involved. But from my experience, if you're willing to put up with a little pain (or in some cases a lot) and make those changes, great things can be accomplished. And believe me, I'm no one special. I have no superhero powers, so if I can make these changes anyone can.

I want you to realize that, even though we're all part of a bigger system that influences us in one way or another, ultimately we're in control of ourselves and the outcomes in our lives. Not politicians, not the news media, not celebrities—it's we who drive the cars of our lives. In the end, we're just simple, hairless apes who want to enjoy what this life has to offer. To me that doesn't mean being 50 pounds overweight, in debt, having no savings for retirement, stressed out, working a job we hate, worrying about how many friends we have and likes we get on social media, and doing what others want us to do (politicians are great at this) instead of the things *we* want to do.

With that said, I want to leave you with my favorite quote from Albert Einstein:

> *Any fool can make things bigger, more complex, and more violent. It takes a touch of genius and a lot of courage to move in the opposite direction.*

1

My Story: How I Decluttered, Minimized and Simplified My Life

In the next couple of chapters, I'll cover how I started on my journey of living a simpler and happier life. I've included this information in some of my previous books, as it outlines my story and the valuable lessons I've learned. For those who've already read my story in my other books, you can skip ahead to Chapter 3 if you so desire. Rereading it, though, might be a good review to light a fire under your butt to get going!

DEALING WITH TODAY'S LIFE GRIND

As most of you who follow me or have read my book *Going Off The Grid* know, my journey didn't start on a whim. I constructed the foundation of how I live now over a decade ago. It started as a desire to live more remotely and simply, then it evolved into a complete lifestyle change.

First, I think it's important to understand that I grew up in a small town in the mountains of California, so living off the grid in the Pacific Northwest is not as drastic a stretch for me as one might think. I didn't go into this adventure completely in the dark.

During my life, I've lived in many cities across the country. As I've gotten older, though, I've become disenchanted with and disengaged from that type of living. Urban living is not a bad lifestyle; it's just not for me anymore.

Having grown up poor, in a single-wide trailer with very few neighbors, you might think I'd never want to return to such a lifestyle. But that couldn't be further from the truth. Growing up that way has given me a unique perspective and shaped my thoughts about what's truly important. Sure, at times things were tough when I was young, but it made me appreciate everything I had that much more. I now look back and consider myself incredibly lucky to have had those experiences. I was fortunate enough to know most of the people in my town and was able to wave at them and get a wave back in return. That's pretty much unheard of in most urban settings today.

I still have fond memories of racing home from football practice before the sun went down to get in an hour of bird hunting. Heck, I would have my shotgun behind the seat of my truck to save time. Yes, that would mean I had a shotgun on school grounds, and I wouldn't have been the only one. A lot of us were hunters, and that was just all there was to it. Can you imagine what would happen to a kid doing that today?

I hate to have to do this, but I must clarify that the above does not represent my personal opinion or political view on gun control. Yep, in today's easily offended society I've felt it necessary to put this paragraph and explanation in. If the above paragraph offends you, or drives you to leave a scathing review of this book based almost purely on it (my story), this book is probably not for you. Or maybe it's exactly what you need. If you're just delirious with anger over this, I would highly recommend you skip to Chapter 12 and read that first. The previous paragraph is a part of my childhood and young adult story, and I refuse to remove it so as not to offend anyone, as some have recommended I do. Well, that's not going to happen, as I won't allow anyone to edit my life story in such a way. OK, I'm done, and off the soapbox I go!

My hunting activity was based on pure simplicity. I didn't wear any special hunting outfit, just the same clothes I wore to school that day. My shotgun was nothing special; it was inexpensive and bought used, and worked just as well as a shotgun ten times the price. I still own and use that shotgun today, nearly 40 years later.

Once I left for college at eighteen, I had very few opportunities to do the things I enjoyed doing while growing up—hiking, fishing, hunting, and just being in nature. And for many years I yearned to return to that type of living. It's hard to explain to someone who's never experienced this lifestyle, but spending time outdoors has always made me the happiest.

To me, the daily grind of living in congested areas has become completely overwhelming and too stressful. Why would I want to sit in traffic if I don't have to? The thought of going to the mall actually makes me cringe, to say the least.

But I can't state this enough: There was a lot of planning required for me to transition to my current lifestyle, with numerous false starts and mistakes made along the way. With that being said, I wouldn't change a thing. Well, maybe I wish someone had already written the books I've put together, as it would have made my life much easier.

Like most people today, I was doing the day-to-day grind. I'd spent almost half my life working for the government in one form or another and was completely burned out and questioning numerous aspects of my life. I remember just sitting there at my desk, after another joyless meeting with one of my bosses, thinking, *What the heck am I doing with my life?* I knew I needed a plan, but what was that plan? I had a house that was ridiculously expensive, with more debt than I wanted or was really necessary, and I was living in congested Southern California, slowly losing my mind.

I remember wondering back then, *Is there something wrong with me?* But since I've changed my lifestyle, I've spoken to and received emails from hundreds and hundreds of people who feel exactly as I did. I now know that the dissatisfaction I had with my previous lifestyle and mindset is not an unusual sentiment. If you feel this way, you're not alone. Today, there are a lot more people who are looking for, or who are actually living, the type of lifestyle I live now. Simply put, we're not willing to accept the modern-day societal expectation that we grind ourselves to oblivion chasing someone else's predefined idea of happiness ... there has to be a better way!

The Search Begins... Kind Of

The original plan began simply with this: I wanted to find someplace quiet to get away to. So I started looking at remote land and cabins in Oregon, Washington, Wyoming, and Montana. At first it was just a cursory look. As it was in the middle of the housing boom, I soon noticed that remote properties were just as overpriced as the typical single-family dwelling in more populated areas. I called a couple of realtors just to get some information, but nothing serious came of it. At that point I was a little discouraged that my plan was nothing more than a dream.

So I shelved my plan and continued with my daily grind, feeling let down and not sure what to do next. What I've now found, after over a decade of research, is that everyone goes through this type of discouragement when they first start trying to make these changes. So don't lose hope.

Another important point I need to make is that I've never fit into the mold of today's typical American lifestyle: the nine-to-five job, the commute, the cookie-cutter suburban home. I started my own side business a good ten years prior to hatching my idea of a mobile lifestyle in an effort to break out, and I've always been more of a free thinker.

I knew that in order to really have freedom, I'd have to run not only my own life but possibly my own business. Let me assure you, though, I don't think it's 100 percent necessary for you to run your own business to live a simpler and more mobile lifestyle—but it sure helps.

The best advice I can give is if you're feeling the grind, and really serious about living a simpler or more mobile life, you need to come up with a business model that fits in with your plans. Today, telecommuting is becoming more common for certain jobs that don't require you to be in an office day-to-day, so just because you have a nine-to-five job doesn't mean you can't simplify and declutter your life.

A Kick in the Butt—The Real Search Begins

Fast-forward to 2013, and all these thoughts were still in the back of my mind. But due to many life-changing circumstances, I wasn't really pursing my dream; I was in a rut. In that year, the stress of trying to run my own business weighed on me, and numerous recent deaths of loved ones, including one of my best friends, hit home. I knew if I kept saying, *I'll get to it next year*, it would never happen.

So with that, I rekindled the dream and put a plan into action. From the time when I had originally thought about living a simpler, more remote lifestyle, my ideas had evolved and changed.

I had started a new business, sold my house and most of my belongings, and was debt free. That put me in a much better place to really pursue my dream.

My original plan was to have a remote getaway; now it was to live off the grid for at least part of the year, dedicating myself to being more mobile rather than stuck in one place. I was fortunate while working in the government to have traveled all over the world, but that lifestyle was addictive. I had caught the nomadic bug and realized I could no longer just stay in one place for very long. In addition, the housing bubble had taught me that the supposed American dream of home ownership—with that big fat mortgage—is a chain around the ankle of a freedom-based lifestyle.

Most think that living a mobile lifestyle, or living off the grid, means living in a beat-up van, cave, or shack with no running water or electricity. Today, that couldn't be further from the truth. You can now live a comfortable life on a piece of fairly isolated land or travel around in a state-of-the-art RV, and I know this for a fact! Not only have I been doing it for years, but I've run into more people than I can count who are doing the same thing or something very similar.

I'm going to address this now, as it's the main argument I get from people who think what I do is not obtainable for most people because I'm single with no kids. I could go into a long diatribe about life decisions and lifestyle choices, but I won't—maybe in another book (ha ha, just kidding.) The fact is, I've met so many people who are married with two to three kids, not to mention multiple pets, who are living *exactly* like I am. I'm telling you with firsthand knowledge, *anyone can live this lifestyle successfully if they want to.* It all boils down to whether you want it and will make it happen proactively, or whether you just want to make excuses and complain about your life. Yes, it's a little tough love, but someone has to say it. This lifestyle is as simple as coming up with a plan and putting it into action, instead of waiting for a miracle to happen, which will more than likely never occur.

I think the best part of this adventure is that I'm funding it in a way most Americans can afford. I don't come from a long line of millionaires, and I don't have unlimited resources. Still, I won't deny that it does cost money, especially in the beginning. I know there are shows and books that say you can just take off with a hundred bucks in your pocket and do it. And some people have done it that way, but I like to live in reality and talk about what's plausible for *most* people, not a select few.

I'm hoping you'll enjoy my adventure, and even if you're not interested in such a lifestyle, maybe you'll learn a little something that you can incorporate into your life to make it simpler and more enjoyable.

2

So Where Do You Start? You Have Too Much Crap!

When you're thinking about simplifying and decluttering your life, I think it's best to have a solid starting point. As I preach in my other books, it's always better to have a plan and to take it slow in the beginning. Many people caught up in our society's instant-gratification thought process forget that great things come with time and perseverance.

As you now know, my life simplification and off-grid journey started several years ago when I decided to downsize. After owning several homes that were much bigger than I needed, and filled with crap I would never use, I decided it was time for a change.

The bottom line is, if you're truly interested in decluttering and simplifying, you're going to have to downsize ... and for most of you, you'll have to downsize big time! Don't be one of those people with a convoy of moving trucks moving all your crap from the city to the country, or getting multiple storage units to hold your hoards of useless items.

CONSUMER NATION: BUYING EVERYTHING IN SIGHT DOESN'T EQUAL HAPPINESS

Like most people today, I had spent my life being just what society and the system wanted me to be: the ultimate consumer. It's no secret that our lives suffer under maximum workloads in order to make money so we can buy as much as we can to fill the unhappiness void. Now, I'm not saying there's no value in work, and I don't begrudge working hard and earning an honest wage, but I do think we have our priorities way out of whack.

Why do we purchase the biggest house we can obtain and shackle ourselves to its suffocating loan? Why do we buy that sports car we really can't afford? Why do we have a closet full of clothes and shoes we hardly wear? In the end, we stress ourselves out so we can obtain all these items, and for what? Exactly! You can't answer that question because there's no logical or reasonable answer.

To me, the answer is simple: We do all of the above, and drive ourselves crazy in the process, because that's what we've been told to do in order to find happiness. So in today's society, stuff equals happiness. Trust me, I followed this mantra with gusto, purchasing all kinds of junk I didn't need.

Stop Being a Crap Collector

So where do you start? Well just like any addict, admit you have a problem. I like to attribute the moniker *junkaholic* to the affliction most of us suffer from today. As a human, it might seem like your primary goal in life is to compile as much useless stuff as you can, and then die among the heaps of your ingloriously obtained items in the hope that someone finds you before one of your pets starts eating your face. OK, I know that's a little over the top, but I think you see my point.

Just as I said above, the starting point is realizing that your life means more than your stuff. You'd be more fulfilled by creating experiences rather than by acquiring shiny items. The luster of objects lasts for a very short time, then you need another shiny object to fill the void.

For me, I just had to realize that less was more. But like my optimal health philosophy, the interpretation of *less* will be different for each individual.

The starting point for me was to greatly downsize my living space. Back then I was paying a ridiculous mortgage for a 1,700-square-foot house in Southern California and losing sleep constantly trying to figure out how to pay for it. I was single and had two dogs. Why I thought I needed this much space, even today, is a mystery to me. Well, not really. I had been brainwashed into thinking bigger was better. Don't borrow a small amount, borrow the absolute maximum you can afford, according to some greedy bank's formula, which is guaranteed to make you poor and them rich. In the end, all it did was stress me out, financially and emotionally, and make me spend a great deal of time on upkeep when I could have been using that time doing something I truly enjoyed.

There's one important point I want to make about our modern maximum-consumption lifestyle: Instead of making us happy, it actually makes us less happy and takes time away from our true passions and the individuals we care about. If that isn't true irony, I don't know what is. We spend a great deal of our lives pursuing the things we've been told will make us happy, but in the end they make us miserable and unfulfilled. Wow, the joke's on us. The great news is that we can change this, and I want to share with you my experience and the steps you can take in order to *happify* (my made-up word) and simplify your life!

EVALUATE YOUR CURRENT LIVING CONDITIONS

The first thing you need to analyze is your current living situation. Can you get by with less living space? I would say almost everyone in this country could answer this with a resounding *yes*!

The first thing I did was simple: I analyzed my monthly cost-of-living expenses. This included my mortgage, insurance, utilities, and general upkeep expenses, and it came out to an astounding $3,500 a month.

For those of you who don't live in California, or one of the more expensive states, you're probably flabbergasted by that amount. Let me tell you, that's cheap in Southern California. Most people I know in California easily spend around $5,000 to $6,000, or more, for what I outlined above. Now that I look back with my "what's-important-to-me" clarity, this was absolutely nuts.

I still had about twenty-seven years left on my mortgage, so that meant I could look forward to spending a total of $1,134,000 (yes, that's over a million dollars) if I maintained that type of lifestyle for the remainder of my mortgage. But here's the kicker: Most of us don't maintain, we upgrade. So for many of us, that total would actually go up.

Basically, we're all capable of being millionaires if we just adjust our lifestyle choices. That's a pretty astounding statement, and I hope you're starting to see the insanity of our consumer-based economy in this country. Here's a little tidbit to clarify the above:

Do you know what amount of annual income is considered to be in the top 1 percent in the world financially? It's $30,000 a year. Do you know that if you live in a place where the minimum wage is $15 an hour, working 40 hours a week comes out to $31,200 a year? By world standards, our poorest in the United States are considered some of the richest people in the world!

Most of you might think my example is rather dramatic, but I assure you, once I got settled in to my new, downsized place, it was anything but. As I outlined, I was living in the typical Southern California residential neighborhood in a home with three bedrooms, two bathrooms, and a two-car garage. For a single guy, this is just way too much space. Heck, I think it's too big for the average family, but that's just my opinion.

Is Renting an Option?

The reason I bring up renting as an option is because it's a good transition if you're a homeowner who's planning to sell. Renting gives you a go-between while you downsize and get your plan together, but it avoids you having to make a big leap. It's getting your toes wet, wading into a simpler life in a smaller dwelling.

Obviously, you don't want to rent a place the same size or bigger than what you have already; you have to downsize, which will force you to get rid of the dogs-playing-poker print on the wall in that dusty man cave. That being said, I do know people who skipped this step, sold the house and all their stuff and never looked back. It all comes down to your goals and lifestyle plans.

After analyzing how much my house cost each month, I decided to take a look at renting and see what made sense. I realized I needed time to get my finances in order, work further on my business, and finalize my plan to simplify my life. The first place I checked out was on Craigslist.com, and I'll tell you, it was very discouraging in the beginning; Renting in California is fairly expensive when compared with the rest of the country. And as I write this, another housing boom is overtaking California, and the prices are even higher than the previous one. I guess some of us never learn from the past.

Not to mention, back when I was looking to rent it was just after the housing bubble had burst (the start of the Great Recession), so everyone was trying to do what I was doing. The glut of prospective renters was pushing rents even higher. The icing on the cake was having two large dogs; most rental owners really don't like pets, and if they do accept them they almost always hit you with a significant up-charge.

So what did that mean? Instead of renting in my general location, I had to cast a wider net in order to find more options. And having pets meant I had to look in more rural areas where people didn't care as much about renting to people who have pets. I began by looking for two-bedroom places, and quickly realized the price difference between what I was currently paying and the prospective rental wasn't large enough to justify this choice.

This forced me to start looking outside my perceived comfort zone. I began investigating studios, granny flats (small apartments attached to houses), and cottages (basically a studio house in which all living space is concentrated in one area as with a studio apartment).

This search led me to an entirely new lifestyle I had never experienced before and simplified my life far more than what I was used to. It's amazing: Having less space forces you to have less stuff, which ultimately makes you happier. I'll be honest, though, I really didn't see that happening in the beginning of my search.

Sometimes you might get lucky and find the place you want right away, but from my experience making such a drastic change takes time. Here's why:

- Unless you've lived this way before, these could be neighborhoods or dwellings you've never experienced.

- You'll probably have to search in new areas that you're unfamiliar with, and determine which works best for you current situation.

Here's the key: Change is often painful in the beginning, and there's no getting around that. You have to realize you're making a major life change, and it might be uncomfortable at first. Most great things in life come with some scrapes and bruises along the way. You're taking what society has told you you must do and turning it upside-down for the most part. This can bring about a lot of rethinking about what makes you happy, some self-doubt, and criticism from those around you. The key is to stay the course and just keep going!

My search for a rental home in Southern California took several months—six to be exact. I did a lot of research and soul-searching during this period, and ultimately it paid off. I found a cottage with a full-size yard located in a rural part of San Diego.

In the end, by being patient I ended up in the nicest place I had found, and it had the lowest rent, to the tune of several hundred dollars! My landlords were also the best I've ever had. When you take your time and are patient, a little luck might come your way.

I will emphasize that when renting you need to really evaluate your landlords just like they're evaluating you. For most, moving is not a pleasant experience, so my philosophy is why do it more than you have to! When I moved into my new-to-me rental in San Diego, I knew I would be there for at least two years, but I ended up living there for over four years.

That's another key thing to think about: How long do you plan to live in this place? Can you stay longer if need be? If you own, will you be able to sell your house in a timely manner, or will you have to try and turn your former home into a rental?

In my situation, I was unsure how long I would be there, but I made sure it was something I could do long-term if I needed to. Thankfully, I had thought that through, because I ended up being in the cottage rental far longer than I had originally expected.

I know most of you who are married and have children are probably thinking, *Yeah, that's no problem for a single guy, but our situation is different.* Well, yes and no. I know families who've reduced their living area by half with no problem at all. Sure, at first they and their kids had to get used to the new lifestyle, but once they adapted, I never heard one complaint about not having enough space. It's all about facing the challenge and not giving in to the sentiment that *it's just too hard.*

Simplifying your life comes with challenges, and you have to keep your eye on the prize at the end. More financial stability and less stuff ultimately means more freedom. I'm not saying that minimizing your living space and having more disposable income is the solution to all your life problems. But I can promise you this: It's easier to figure them out without additional self-perpetuated stress.

The Payoff

The 2008 recession was not kind to most of us. I'll be honest, I ended up selling my house for a significant loss, but I had to make a critical choice: Let the house eventually push me into bankruptcy, or sacrifice short-term loss for long-term happiness. These were incredibly tough circumstances, but I don't regret what I did for a second.

The payoff for me was undeniable. By forcing myself way out of my comfort zone I found a great rental home for a great price. Now I know you're wondering, *So how big was the cottage?* My new rental place was around 475 square feet (based on my measurements). That's right, I went from 1,700 to 475 square feet—almost a 75 percent reduction in living space!

Do I recommend everyone make such a drastic change? Of course not. Again, it depends on your situation and your comfort levels. I will tell you that I have no regrets and the thought of ever living in a big house again has not once crossed my mind since I made the change. And I draw the above advice from my real-life experience. As most of you know from my other books, I never give you advice about things I haven't done myself.

Now let's get down to the nitty-gritty—how much did I save? I was able to go from $3,500 in basic living expenses per month to $1,100 a month. And the best part for me was not just saving a lot of money, but also not having all the stress of maintaining and paying for a large house. That was priceless.

Another bonus was that I had to sell a lot of stuff because there was no way it was going to fit into the rental cottage. I made close to $10,000 selling all my extra crap on Craigslist, and I sold most of it in 48 hours! I can't explain the cleansing effect this had on my psyche and life. After selling all those useless possessions, it felt as if a huge weight had been lifted off my shoulders.

I've learned that modern home ownership not only costs you financially, but it can also put you in a situation where you can get stuck. I used my time in the rental place to plot out my next move (which turned out to be my mobile lifestyle and off-the-grid project!) and make sure I wasn't rushing into anything I would later regret. I know not everything can be planned for, nor does everything always work out perfectly, but I like to give myself the best odds possible to avoid as many pitfalls as I can.

Operation Travel Trailer: Hello, Tiny Living

As I explained above, this renting period taught me how to downsize; it also bought me time to get my ultimate plan together. By the time I'd been renting for about three years, I had purchased twenty acres of land for my off-grid house project. I was ready for the next step.

I found that while building a house off the grid, a great way to enjoy the property and save money is to live in an RV on the property. As a matter of fact, I've since learned that this is how most people build an off-grid house. Because there's usually no financing for off-grid homes, it typically takes three to five years to complete the project. The upside is that you usually have no, or very little, debt when it's done; the downside is that you need someplace to live for the duration. (For those interested in the off-grid lifestyle, I highly recommend you get my book *Going Off The Grid*, as it's a step-by-step how-to-book.) For me, I planned to live the mobile *and* off-the-grid lifestyle, so I now needed to get a travel trailer.

Whoops, A Snag In Operation Travel Trailer

As I said in the beginning, I share it all, good and bad. I thought I had the perfect strategy living on my property in my travel trailer until I built my house. But this is where my inexperience with travel trailers bit me in the butt. At this time I had a 4x4 V6 Toyota Tacoma, and my travel trailer was an 18' Ultra Lite which is made to be towed by smaller vehicles. There were a few problems with my plan, though:

- My property has terrible roads

- The roads are very steep

- My truck at the time didn't have anywhere near the power to tow a trailer in those conditions

- If I was able to get the travel trailer to the property, there was no way I was getting it out

Luckily, I decided to do some recon before I towed my trailer up, and I realized my original plan wasn't going to work. Did I panic? Well, maybe a little, but what that did was make me look around for RV parks. I found there were more than enough in the area, and they ended up costing me only about $300 a month. I stayed at two different RV parks while building my house, and to be honest it wasn't bad and made running my business while building the house a lot easier than it could have been.

In the end, my mistake ended up being a blessing in disguise. During the time of towing my trailer around, I realized I really enjoyed this type of mobile lifestyle. To this day, I still own my travel trailer and spend half the year living in it and traveling around.

I know the story above focuses on my process building my off-grid house, but as you can see it required a big-time decluttering of my life. During this process I had to sell a lot of items that were unnecessary, downsize, get my finances in order, and find my path in life. But there were a lot of other pieces that were important, and are essential to my current and continuing journey.

In the following chapters I'll be identifying what I think are the biggest life issues that must be addressed. I think you'll be surprised by a few of them, as I know a lot of books on the topics of life simplification and decluttering don't cover these important pieces of the puzzle. Now, I'm not saying you need to do what I've done. This is *your* journey, and everyone goes about it their own way. But I feel that sharing my own story will help you gain some perspective about what life simplification and decluttering can do for you.

3

The Five Key Principles for Living *The Simple Life*

It's hard to believe I came up with the Five Key Principles For Living *The Simple Life* almost a decade ago, while working with clients starting on their path to optimal health. I consider the below principles to be the cornerstone and primary philosophy of everything I teach. I didn't come up with these out of thin air; they came from decades of trial and error, not only in my own life but also while working with others. I've found that following these five key principles keeps everything in perspective and allows me to focus on the things that are truly important when changing my life for the positive. As a matter of fact, I consider these so important in *your* journey that I highly recommend you print them out and put them somewhere where you'll see them every day.

1. Knowledge is power

2. Avoid extremes

3. Keep it simple

4. Something is better than nothing

5. Take action, today and every day

PRINCIPLE 1: KNOWLEDGE IS POWER

As you read this material, you may wonder why I've taken the time to go over *why* to do things and not just *what* to do. Well, it's because changing your life for the better long-term is not about fads or quick fixes. In today's society we love the easy button. The problem is, there is no easy button in life. Moreover, I have a simple philosophy when it comes to anything in life: *Knowledge is power.* When you have correct, in-depth information, you'll see that making positive changes in your life is far simpler to accomplish and maintain. Instead of following some list by a supposed expert, you can understand the *why* and apply it to your goals and situation in life.

What isn't simple is trying to change decades of bad decisions based on bad information. Almost every day another article or news program promotes a means to living the easy life, yet most of the information is just flat-out wrong, often dangerous, and sometimes a bit of both.

Following advice you don't fully understand rarely results in success. Instead, new habits are most effective when you know *why* you're doing them. Otherwise, you're likely to be swayed by the next fad or miracle product that comes along, without really understanding how it works (or more likely, that it doesn't). Fads are often shrouded in vague pseudo-science and cheesy ads; I want you to have the truth about how to change your life, from someone who has been there and done that!

PRINCIPLE 2: AVOID EXTREMES

Any time I hear a phrase like, "Work just a couple of hours a week and make millions!" or, "[Insert product here] will cure your blues and make you feel good about yourself," I get really ticked off. Why? Because extreme claims may sound appealing, but they're rarely true. They're just to get you to buy something you don't need, or follow a BS philosophy that has no basis in reality. While less sexy and instant-gratification appealing, a slow-and-steady approach with a well-thought-out plan that's followed day after day, week after week, delivers true change for the positive. Extreme actions with very little thought put into them never work out very well in the long term.

Nevertheless, just like everyone else I've fallen victim to numerous fads and promises of easy living during my life. One of the most vivid memories I have from trying to improve my health (a favorite place for hucksters to sell you crap) is of a younger version of myself waking up two or three times a night with a friend to do hundreds of push-ups, sit-ups, pull-ups and other exercises, in addition to eating thousands of additional calories our bodies could never process. It sounded like a good idea at the time, but the results begged to differ—we just ended up fat and tired!

From such experiences I've learned a very important lesson: A fad is merely a fad for a reason, and has no place in the continued pursuit of genuine happiness and a sense of accomplishment. Its main focus is to sell you something short-term. The purveyors of such works-for-the-moment scams don't care if their product or system works for the long term or not. And when the trick-of-the-month doesn't work, or stops working, guess who's ready to sell you the next miracle product?

Change only comes with hard work and dedication to making that change. Avoiding extremes is an important part of getting there.

PRINCIPLE 3: KEEP IT SIMPLE

As a culture, we've turned the concept of living a healthy, happy life into a confusing and overwhelming selection of products, fads and gimmicks.

Have you ever run into someone who has found that "zone" in their life, where they seem content and relaxed, and are just flat-out enjoying themselves? Most people might think those individuals are spending all their waking hours reading blogs, measuring and weighing their food, working out like an Olympic athlete, and using every technology-based gizmo promising simplicity, but in reality that couldn't be further from the truth.

You'll find that the famous "less is more" saying is not just a tagline, but is based in reality. I hope from my above story and path to living a simpler life, you're starting to see that *addition by subtraction* is the key. We love to overthink everything and make living the life we want far more complicated than it needs to be. Trust me I've been there. Once you cut out all the noise and clutter, though, everything starts to come into focus.

PRINCIPLE 4: SOMETHING IS BETTER THAN NOTHING

At first, overhauling your entire lifestyle can seem daunting, especially if you've really let it get out of hand. But here's a thought that always bears repeating: *Little changes and choices add up.* When it comes to doing nothing versus doing at least something, something is always the right choice. Think of it like dropping a dollar into a piggy bank every hour of the day for years and years ... eventually you'd have a nice nest egg. You can always do *something*! Instead of bemoaning your stressful and unfulfilling life, answer this question: What would it take to make a better choice in this situation, at this exact moment? Even if it's only an incrementally better option, that little bit counts!

Do you struggle with money at the end of every month? Analyze your spending habits and figure out a way to save more, no matter how small the amount may be in the beginning.

Hate your job? Take training courses that will allow you to start your own company, or develop skills to find a job you'll enjoy.

Can't get to the gym? Do 10 minutes of push-ups, crunches and stretches in your living room. Even a few push-ups are better than none!

Sit at a desk all day with an aching back? Make it a point to stand up and move around each hour—even if only for two or three minutes!

Exhausted and haven't seen your kids all day? Turn off the TV and catch up together on a brisk walk around the neighborhood (yes, they may complain, but try it anyway!)

When circumstances aren't ideal, don't assume you have no control. You always do. So instead of feeling bad that you can't do *everything*, do something!

PRINCIPLE 5: TAKE ACTION, TODAY AND EVERY DAY

Look, America is full of people who *want* to live a better and more fulfilling life, but in reality very few ever take action to accomplish this. The difference between the people who dream about it and those who reach their goals is continuous action.

Here's the simplest answer: Happy, successful people take action, today and every day. Their lives are an answer to the question: What's it going to take to stay on track and make progress today? Maybe that means getting up a bit earlier to get to the gym, or writing that novel you've talked about for the last ten years. Maybe it means selling that sports car you really can't afford and buying something more practical. Small choices add up to a lifestyle that dictates long-term success. That's the real-world truth.

So, what's it going to take for you to take action today? Every day? This ties into *Principle 4: Something is Better Than Nothing.* If you can't get everything done you set out to accomplish today, this week or this year, do something. Don't give up and say it's just too hard. Don't let things not going exactly as you planned be an excuse for doing nothing. Always ask, *if I can't do the ideal, what else can I do?*

What do you do if your car breaks down and ruins your savings plan for the next couple of months? Go back to saving when the repairs are paid for, and maybe put additional money away for unexpected car repairs in the future.

No time for a full workout today? How about taking the stairs instead of the elevator at every opportunity this week?

Life gets hard, and making better choices is sometimes inconvenient. Want to live debt free or improve your health? The secret is to make the right choices, slowly and surely, today and every day. Today's choices matter, and are under your control, every day.

That's the hard truth. But the good news is, once it's a habit it gets easier. Taking action is always the key.

I think you can now see that the Five Principles for Living *The Simple Life* are based upon developing positive and consistent habits. Short-term fixes never work long term; you must ingrain and practice positive habits to achieve positive outcomes … and it's truly that simple. One thing I can guarantee: If you don't follow the five principles I've outlined, and develop positive life habits, success is going to be very difficult, if not impossible.

Finding Your Purpose:
The Life-Long Question,
"Why Am I Here?"

Before I dive into the meat of decluttering your life, I need to bring up the topic of *purpose*. The most common factor I find causing distress and overall unhappiness for people in today's modern society is a lack of purpose.

So what do I mean by *purpose*? When talking about purpose I'm referring to life purpose. Life purpose is putting into action the things that are not only meaningful to you, but to others as well.

I want you to understand that you don't need to find your purpose right this instant, but it would be good to start thinking about it as you read through the remainder of this material.

I wish I had the magic sauce when it comes to determining purpose, but I don't. Finding your purpose is highly individualistic, as there are many factors that must be considered such as:

- What are you passionate about?

- What's your living situation—married, single, kids or a caregiver?

- Why are you doing what you're doing?

- Where are you at in your life right now?

- What are your current and future goals?

The primary point to realize while trying to find your purpose is that it's not static. In fact, for most it will be a moving target. And very rarely does someone come into this world immediately knowing his or her purpose.

Finding your purpose is done with action—by doing things and by experiencing life and the world. For some, it's being the best mother or father they can be. For others, like Elon Musk, it's being one of the most innovative people in our lifetime. When it comes to purpose there's no right or wrong answer, but I've found for people to truly be happy and fulfilled it's the one thing that must be found.

Just like many others, I floundered early on in my life try-ing to find my purpose. I always knew it was helping people in some shape or form, so that's how I ended up in the military, law enforcement, health, and teaching. But trust me, I'm no life clairvoyant. My purpose has changed and evolved as time has gone by, but it's always been firmly rooted in helping others through my experiences and knowledge. When I first started out as an entrepreneur two decades ago, I would have been shocked if someone had told me my purpose today would be primarily as a self-help author!

A big lesson I've learned in life is that purpose can't be forced; it has to be found organically. For some this comes early in life, for some much later. Your life experiences are going to create and shape your purpose. For example, a friend of mine started out in the stressful world of consulting for technological companies, but he soon found it to be unfulfilling. During this time he was volunteering and working with underprivileged children on the side, and this is where he found his purpose. He left his high-paying job to work for a non-profit helping underprivileged children and never looked back.

Another friend of mine spent a large part of his life in the military special forces. Now retired, he spends a great deal of time working with severely injured veterans and their families. I'm not saying he didn't have purpose in the military, but once he left it shifted into something a little different, but still related to his prior primary purpose.

As humans, we're all truly interconnected. It's not one large act that makes the difference, but many small acts of passion and love for others that bring about change for the better. When it comes to purpose, it's not about collecting items (as we're often taught today), it's about action. That's why *Principle 5: Take Action Today and Every Day* is so important.

You're not going to find your purpose in a shopping mall, by owning a mansion filled with expensive items, or by playing video games (playing video games for a living, sorry, is not a purpose). Purpose is not found in self-absorbed actions or motives. Purpose is found in the greater good—making a difference, no matter how small that difference may be.

As humans, we've evolved into something foreign in relationship to our DNA and past. Humans are tribal and are nurturing by nature, meaning we've historically relied upon each other for survival. We did this by being a part of small groups (usually less than 50 people), where our primary purpose was providing the things we were good at in order to enhance survival and the ability to thrive in this group or tribe. Your purpose in the past may have been to be a hunter to provide the necessary food, or to provide medicine as a healer. It was also possible to have more than one purpose or a sub-purpose.

One thing that was not, and would not be, accepted by our nomadic tribal ancestors was selfishness and hoarding of any type of resource. The emphasis of the individual, and of consumerism, is something very new to the human species. You may now see why so many struggle to find their purpose in today's society, as it's hard to find your purpose when you're primarily focused on only yourself. I believe if this type of behavior was allowed in our past tribal lifestyle, we wouldn't be here today. That famous saying "it takes a village" comes to mind when thinking about the evolution and progress of humans.

Anthropologist Richard Lee noted in 1968 when studying the Kung people of the Kalahari Desert (northern Namibia and southern Angola) who were still living the hunter-gatherer life-style at this time:

> *The members move out each day to hunt and gather, and return in the evening to pool the collected foods in such a way that every person present receives an equita-ble share ... Because of the strong emphasis on sharing, and frequency of movement, surplus accumulation ... is kept to a minimum.*

The above shows that we have traditionally had purpose and belonged to a community, and would not collect unnecessary items just for the sake of having more things.

What I've found while working at being more self-reliant, and belonging to a like-minded group, is that it's about going back to a more primitive lifestyle and being part of a much smaller community. In a way, we consider the way we live to be a tribe—much more communal and focused on helping each other than most types of groups. Later in this book I'll discuss the importance of finding your tribe and decluttering your relationships.

You might find that some of your current relationships can be detrimental to you finding your purpose, as can worrying about what other people think. I've found this to be incredibly true in the area of health. Once someone sets out on their journey to be healthier, family or friends can sometimes try to sabotage or dissuade him or her from pursuing this goal. I've seen it time and time again while working with clients. For you to find your purpose, you might have to ignore what other people think and say. After all, this is *your* purpose in life, not theirs.

After leaving the government, starting my primal health business, and transitioning to a simpler life, my friends and family thought I was nuts. A couple of friends actually pulled me aside and asked me if I was OK. Others flat-out made fun of me and what I was trying to accomplish in pursuit of my life purpose. If I had let what they were saying influence my decisions at that time, you wouldn't be reading these words today.

Here's the amazing thing about living a simpler, more altruistic life: Either you'll find your purpose or your purpose will find you. But here are a couple of questions I'll leave you with in order to help those who are struggling to find their purpose:

- If you could do anything that didn't require you to make money, what would that be?

- When you die, what do want to be remembered for? (I'm pretty sure it's not having the most friends on Facebook!)

Being a realist, I have to admit that having a purpose alone is not going to pay the bills or feed your family. In today's society we need to have a balance between having purpose and supplying our minimal survival needs. With that being said, I think most people can weave their purpose into their primary source of income. I know this firsthand because I've done it myself and have taught many others to do the same.

DECLUTTERING YOUR HEALTH:
The Biggest Elephant in the Room!

Some are probably scratching their heads right now thinking, *What does my health have to do with making my life simpler and happier?* I'll say with 100 percent confidence: everything! I've been involved in the areas of health and athletics for over four decades, and I've come to the conclusion that our declining health is the biggest factor (just behind life purpose) in our overall lack of life satisfaction and happiness. It all starts with your health, and if you don't make this your number one priority in the pursuit of simple living, everything else I'll cover in this book will be far, far more difficult to implement.

This section will not be an all-inclusive guide on how to get healthy. My book *The Simple Life Guide To Optimal Health: How to Get Healthy, Lose Weight, Reverse Disease and Feel Better Than Ever* is an A-to-Z guide to nutrition, exercise and supplementation. My main goal here is to educate you on why your health is the main key to living the life you want.

Over the last decade I've worked with a large number of individuals in finding their path to optimal health. From this experience I can tell you that two main things are derailing people from achieving their life goals and acquiring happiness: health and financial stability. We'll discuss finances in the next chapter, but I want to get you thinking about your health first, as it's incredibly important and one of simplest things to fix.

HOW TO FIND AN OBESE PERSON—IT ONLY TAKES ABOUT 30 SECONDS TODAY!

During the last five years I've noticed Americans are growing (round, not tall) at an alarming rate. After talking to some other individuals in the realm of health, I asked them if they were witnessing the same thing as I was, and to my surprise all said yes.

With this observational information I decided to run a little experiment. For the last year, no matter where I've been, I've stopped for a bit to observe the people around me to see how long it would take me to find an individual who was obese. There were no prerequisites (age, gender, race, etc.), other than whether or not they appeared to be obese.

Obesity today is primarily determined by our Body Mass Index (BMI). BMI is calculated by taking a person's weight in kilograms and dividing it by the square of their height in meters, but BMI does not measure body fat directly.

Obviously, I didn't use the above parameter in my experiment, as I couldn't ask the person I observed to come over and let me measure them to determine their BMI. But with my experience in health, I've got a pretty good idea of what people should weigh in relation to their height. Of course, this is not a highly scientific study, but I'm using it to show you just how much our health is in decline today. I used a general guideline that would categorize someone as obese if they appeared to be around fifty or more pounds overweight.

When I first started this experiment, I knew it wouldn't be very difficult to find people I considered obese, but what I actually found was truly shocking. On average, it took me less than 30 seconds, and usually less than 10 seconds, to find someone I would categorize as obese. What I really didn't expect is that in most cases I found them to be what I would consider to be morbidly obese (100 pounds or more overweight).

What also blew me away was the amount of people I saw that I would consider to be able-bodied but who were severely overweight and rolling around in electric scooters. From what I observed, they had no physical condition or disability, other than being overweight, that would cause them to have to use a scooter.

Folks, we don't just have a problem, we have a full-blown epidemic on our hands!

Now, if you're taking the above as some sort of fat shaming or being insensitive, this book is not for you. If you have a problem with honest observation in order to deal with an important issue and come up with a solution, I can't help you.

This book was written to help people who are looking to make positive changes in their lives. And in order to make changes, you need to identify the problem(s) and solve them—plain and simple. Change for the better can be painful; most lessons in life are learned from things that don't come easy, through struggle, and by not giving up.

Your health is not only about feeling better and looking good in a bathing suit. I believe it affects almost everything in your life such as:

Psychological well-being
Cognitive function

Ability to interact with others

Attitude

Mood

Endurance

Relationships

Sex drive

Financial success

Ability to deal with stress

Health of your offspring

Quality of sleep

Energy levels

Creativity

Ability to learn

Ability to focus

I hope you can now see why your health is so important. Your health is the one thing that you can change right here, right now. And once you control your health, you've taken a huge step in controlling everything else in your life.

The unfortunate thing is that the way our (be-the-ultimate-consumer) society is devised today, things are stacked against us. During the many interviews I've done over the years I've often said, "There's no money in healthy people!" Take a moment to think of all the agencies, institutions and businesses that make billions by us not being healthy and relying on them to dictate how our health should be navigated. I have some enemies in the health world because what I teach takes money from these immoral beasts.

BEING OVERWEIGHT IS NOT A DISEASE, IT'S A LIFE CHOICE

Now that I've offended some of you (maybe more than once at this point), let me clarify something. If I had a nickel for every person I've consulted with on their health that told me "I have a bad metabolism, I'm big boned, etc.," I would be a very rich man. When it comes to excuses, health has to be ranked #1 in the "it's not my fault" category.

We've become so soft and gooey in today's society that we pretty much have an excuse for everything. I know, as I've used them myself. We now call obesity and being overweight a disease, but I can't say it any plainer than this: Making poor life choices in the area of health is not a disease! How we've decided that eating poorly and not getting enough exercise is somehow a disease is appalling to me. Society has given us a built-in excuse to waddle through life—don't address the problem, just buy a pair of stretchy pants and blame everyone else!

Disease is defined as: an illness of people, animals, plants, etc., caused by infection or a failure of health rather than by an accident. I'm pretty sure donuts don't fall into our mouths by accident, and our butts aren't the size of a 4X4 truck tire because of an infection! Now there are some people who are born with, or acquire, condition(s) that cause them to be overweight or obese, but I'll tell you they're very, very rare. Yes, it's becoming more common today, but guess why? Because we're passing down poor genetics caused by improper diet and exercise, thus making the problem worse. And here's the catch: Your poor diet and expanding waistline can *cause* disease, but eating poorly and neglecting exercise is not a disease. We've greatly confused cause and effect when it comes to our health and disease.

THE OVERWEIGHT STATE OF OUR NATION

During my younger years, I was very physically active and managed to maintain a healthy weight despite consuming a terribly unhealthy diet. However, since most of us move less as we age, adjustments to diet must be made as we get older to avoid disease, illness, pain, and depression. In other words, proper nutrition must ultimately be addressed to avoid an unhappy and unhealthy you in the teenage years and beyond.

Even though your upbringing is just one factor that may play a role in your current physical condition, there seem to be other major contributors to the increasingly heftier and unhealthier American population

For instance, did you know the average grocery store has in the neighborhood of 45,000 items? We're in a state of over-stimulation and confusion when it comes to our health and diet. It would take you nearly 125 years to consume them if you bought one of these 45,000 items each day. And if you think this is done by accident you would be wrong.

There are billions of dollars spent every year on determining where and how to place these items to get you to purchase something you really don't need, and which in most cases will not benefit your health. Do you ever wonder why those energy drinks, gossip magazines, and candy are next to the checkout aisle? Because you're far more likely to impulse buy them when standing in line.

And here's true irony: Today we buy more cookbooks and watch more healthy cooking shows than any time in our history, but we cook our own meals at the lowest rate ever.

Is it starting to be become clear why it's estimated that 40 percent of Americans are considered obese, with some estimates even higher than that? And it's predicted that by 2030 over half of the American population will be considered obese if we continue on our current path.

Why are over sixty percent of us overweight? According to the 2014 Centers for Disease Control (CDC) State Indicator on Physical Activity, over 25 percent of Americans are completely sedentary, meaning they perform or participate in *no* physical activity in their daily lives. Now that's scary! No wonder U.S. healthcare costs are rising at an alarming rate.

Even more surprising is the statistical life expectancy of the average American, as ranked in the 2017 *Central Intelligence Agency* (CIA) *World Fact Book* estimates. America is widely considered to be the world's beacon of prosperity, to have the most advanced health care system, and to have the most efficient and productive agricultural system in the world. Yet when looking at the U.S. life expectancy rating, you would think those statements were complete fiction, and that the U.S. must be a struggling third world country. Shockingly, when considering longevity, we're not even among the top ten countries worldwide. We barely make the top fifty; *we're, in fact, ranked a miserable forty-third in the world.*

The estimated life expectancy of an American is 80 years, which is over nine years *less* than the country with the longest-living residents: Monaco. When compared to Americans, it's the citizens of Bermuda, Malta, South Korea, and Jordan (to name only a few examples) who may anticipate a longer life. It's amazing that we give large sums of financial and military support to a country such as South Korea, yet its citizens have a higher life expectancy than the average American.

The *CIA World Fact Book* notes that:

> *Life expectancy at birth is also a measure of over-*
> *all quality of life in a country and summarizes the*

mortality at all ages. It can also be thought of as indicating the potential return on investment in human capital and is necessary for the calculation of various actuarial measures.

I believe that health is a critical element of the future prosperity of our country. Yet in America, we're not only losing the battle for health, we're also losing it at an alarming rate. We pride ourselves in being number one ... congratulations, we're one of the most obese countries in the world, and number one in North America!

No other country spends as much on healthcare as the United States. In 2017 healthcare spending in the U.S. accounted for 17.1 percent of the Gross Domestic Product (GDP), according to the Organization for Economic Co-Operation and Development (OECD). And according to some estimates, this number could be as high as 25 percent by 2020.

In 2017 the United States spent $10,209 on health per person, a figure more than double Japan's $4,717 per person, which is ranked second in the world for life expectancy from birth. Americans also spent over twice as much as Europe's wealthiest countries in total, per person, including France and the United Kingdom.

Despite these dismal figures, our nation has access to more knowledge than ever before about health and wellness. The growing use of technology puts data and research at our fingertips in an instant. We now have more health and nutrition centers available to us, and organic foods are now offered at many local grocery stores. We also have greater access to an astonishing array of supplements and vitamins. And local gyms have made it more convenient to squeeze a workout into your busy day.

The U.S. healthcare debate is in full swing as I write this. Would this topic even be an issue if our citizens were healthy, eating well and exercising? It wouldn't; this issue would be mostly irrelevant, and we could easily ensure the less fortunate could receive health care without financially devastating our country.

How is it possible that the citizens of countries who are literally decades behind us in terms of technological development live longer than most Americans? Simply, they take their health far more seriously than we do.

I believe we're on the brink of a new health awakening in America. At least I hope we are. If not, the burden of our increasing healthcare needs will usher in an era of increasing fiscal debt—and possibly financial disaster. Healthcare costs currently account for one sixth of the American economy and are growing at an alarming pace. This is not a fleeting crisis; it has the potential to greatly inhibit our social and economic growth for current and future generations.

Our Childrens' Health and Future at Risk

But the toll goes further than money. The White House website now indicates that some politicians are encouraging doctors to write medical prescriptions for obese children as young as 8 years old (who are really in need of exercise and whole, natural foods).

If this unwanted interjection into our childrens' health by the U.S. government doesn't awaken and frighten the average American, I don't know what will. First, let's consider the implications of prescribing drugs for overweight children.

I believe that prescribing medications for a condition (obesity) that can, in most cases, be completely remedied through proper exercise and nutrition is both irresponsible and immoral.

We've now come to the point where we give our children drugs instead of a wellness-based education. To this day, I've yet to see an overweight child or adult who eats plenty of fruits, vegetables, protein and healthy fats, and who exercises regularly. Prescribing drugs for obesity is akin to treating a symptom instead of the causative problem.

It's much easier to teach children about exercise and fitness than it is to instruct them in healthy nutrition. Children have the natural instinct to run, chase, dodge, hide, kick and play. It's easy to take a ball from your garage and imagine, invent and create new games to play with your neighborhood friends. As children we may have asked an adult to teach us how to play football, but never to teach us the right way to eat.

The good news: If over the years you've developed an unhealthy relationship with food—or with your unhealthy self—you can reverse it! It's time to turn unhealthy behaviors into health-giving habits.

THE WESTERN DIET—WE LOVE SPREADING OUR MISERY!

The Western Diet has probably caused more death, health problems, and unnecessary expenditures on health ailments than any diet known to modern humans. You've likely heard this term many times, but you may not understand what it actually entails. The Western Diet is typically eaten in developed (and some developing) countries throughout the world. It's heavily weighted toward large amounts of processed foods and factory-farmed meat, large quantities of added unhealthy fats and oils, sugars, and refined grains. Fruits, vegetables and unprocessed, fresh foods of any type are largely lacking.

Populations who eat the standard Western Diet tend to suffer from high rates of obesity, type 2 diabetes (a lifestyle disease not to be confused with type 1 diabetes, which is an autoimmune condition), and cardiovascular disease. And some research indicates that more than a third of all cancers can be linked to this way of eating.

But there are more health problems associated with the Western Diet. Industrially produced foods prevalent in the developed world frequently contain unnatural chemicals and hormones. Recent research from the Cincinnati Children's Hospital Medical Center has shown that young girls are starting to undergo puberty earlier—some as young as seven or eight years old. These chemical "endocrine disruptors" are also implicated in other metabolic disorders involving thyroid dysfunction, mood impairment, and more.

Does the Western Diet sound like your way of eating? I know it used to be mine. How did we learn to eat this way? From our schools, popular cookbooks, government food recommendations, or our family? Perhaps it was a bit of each. What's certain is that the typical Western Diet leads to impaired health and an earlier demise than do the eating habits of poorer, less developed countries, where the diet is still based on fresh, clean, and unprocessed traditional foods.

Thanks to some medical advances, we do live longer than we used to. But what's the real benefit if our added years are largely spent in and out of hospitals or not feeling well? Who wants to be wasting away for years with cancer due to a condition caused by the Western Diet? I know I don't! Our advances in medicine, health care, and science are exciting, but relying on them to prolong an unhealthy life is not the answer. Even though an individual may live longer than his forebears, if he's sick and miserable it's no blessing for him or his family and community!

But there is good news. Years of research now indicate that the effects of the Western Diet can, for the most part, be reversed. Studies have shown that people who've abandoned the Western

Diet for a more traditional and natural diet will regain health and reduce their chances of suffering from the usual Western Diet-induced chronic diseases.

Shockingly, the first known study on the negative consequences of the Western Diet pre-dates World War II! Such important nutritional information has been known for almost one hundred years or more. Why is it not taught in our schools and nutrition courses, or disseminated in literature produced by our government?

Now, you may feel resistant to changing the way you eat. You may be thinking, *Why don't I just exercise more to take care of my current weight and health problems?* The reason that approach won't work is that diet adjustments *and* exercise when combined yield exponential and powerful results. Trust me, every year people make the ever-so-popular New Year's resolution to join a gym and try to exercise away their poor health choices—it simply doesn't work!

Being Healthy—So Easy A Caveman Could Do It

One straightforward tool when teaching people how to get healthy, and do it simply, is the concept of prehistoric man/woman. Modern humans evolved consuming a diet of natural foods based on actively gathering plant-based foods and hunting animals (hunter-gatherer). Our bodies, though highly adaptive, need specific nutrients that can only be found in nature to function properly. This has been the case for millions of years and for far longer than our modern ways of eating have existed. This nutritional paradigm has only changed in the last few hundred years, thanks to the advent of industrialized agriculture and factory food production.

The prehistoric man/woman concept is an easy tool to use when you become confused about food or health choices. If the modern world as you know it were to end, and you had to live off of the land like our predecessors, what would you eat? What foods would you have access to in your immediate area?

Whenever you have a question about your food selections, just think what a prehistoric man or woman would have had as food choices. Would they have had access to sweet flavored water, processed starchy pasta, high-fructose corn syrup, sugary breakfast cereals, or artificial sweeteners?

And did prehistoric man/woman worry about saturated fat? Humans before us didn't concern themselves with counting calories or our other modern dietary concerns. They just ate what was naturally in abundance around them, when they were hungry.

Some skeptics may say that the life expectancy of the average prehistoric human was actually quite short, and they argue that this throws doubt on the health benefits of our early ancestors' way of living. However, their life spans were no doubt affected by other circumstances, such as high risk of death by trauma and injury. Our prehistoric brethren were not at the top of the food chain; they were themselves hunted by large predators and didn't always enjoy the constant abundance of food that we have today. Remember, a fat, slow caveman is just an easy, tasty meal for another predator!

Moreover, they would not have necessarily lived by the rules of law that aim to protect us today and would have fought vicious battles against neighboring tribes and groups—and sometimes against each other. They lived a much harsher and more violent life than modern humans, and thus died for many reasons that are far outside the scope of mere nutrition. Had they had constant access to readily available foods, and had they not had to suffer so many stresses inherent in their everyday survival, fewer would have died at an early age. Indeed, in such idealized circumstances, many prehistoric humans would have lived far longer—possibly longer than we do today.

In a similar way, consider the life span of your house pet. Would your furry friend live as long in the wild as it would in your home, where constant shelter, food, and healthcare are provided? Clearly, many factors no longer relevant to modern life must be considered when reflecting upon the average life expectancy of early humans.

Eating should be simple. If you pick up a food product in a grocery store and it contains ingredients you can't pronounce, or a list of ingredients so long that it takes up an entire side of the container, it's probably a bad choice. Plus, I'm pretty sure it would not be recognized as a food by our prehistoric ancestors. Keep this thought in mind.

I often get asked, "If I wasn't intended to eat sweets, salty and greasy foods why do I crave them so much?" When trying to answer this question, you have to look at yourself (a human) for what you truly are (an animal) and where you came from—a hunter-gatherer living amongst other animals.

Finding highly caloric sweets in nature was very difficult and usually only in the form of fruits; if you were really lucky you might find some honey. Today we've removed ourselves from the animal kingdom, thus we forget we weren't the only thing (think predators, some very fast and large ones at that) looking for these sweet sources of food.

Simply, because of this rarity of high calorie sweet foods, we're wired within our DNA to gorge ourselves on these hard-to-find foods as a survival mechanism. That's why our stomachs can stretch to accommodate this gorging when necessary.

Today we live in a state of plenty, especially when it comes to food. Just one aisle in your grocery store filled with nutrient-empty cookies, cakes, juices and sodas contains more sweets than you would be exposed to in your entire life as a hunter-gatherer. Our livestock today is raised to have the highest amount of fat content possible, and the fact that they're far less active than they would be in the wild means they have less dense muscle mass as well. Anyone who's hunted knows a wild animal's muscle-to-fat ratio is far different from the domesticated animals of today. But that's not to say fat is necessarily bad for you.

The Solution?

I know I just threw a lot of information at you outlining the problem, but *Gee, Gary, what's the solution?* I'm not going to cover everything you need to implement in this book because it would be far too long. I'm a big fan of writing shorter books, so you can remember and implement the information right away. If you're someone who's struggling with your health, though, and you'd like more information on how to turn it around. I go over that subject in great detail in my book *The Simple Life Guide to Optimal Health.*

With that said, I want to give you ten things to start thinking about and implementing below:

1. Identify your health problems and determine what you need to do to change them

2. Schedule into your life at least five hours of physical activity a week

3. Learn how to cook your own food (not donuts and crap—healthy food)

4. Find people with the same healthy mindset and goals as you

5. Find your motivation

6. Identify what types of exercise you enjoy

7. Stop blaming others

8. Get 7 to 8 hours of sleep per night

9. Remove unnecessary stressors

10. Stop whining and get it done!

OVERCOMING YOUR INTERNAL RESISTANCE

As final inspiration, I'd like to defer to the words of author Steven Pressfield in his book, *The War of Art*. Pressfield's book is primarily focused on the professional struggles of writers as they produce the written word. But Pressfield's words and ideas on "resistance" can also be applied to the challenges of nutritional and physical health. I've read *The War of Art* several times during times of struggle to light a fire under my butt, so I highly recommend it.

Here are some of my favorite passages:

Have you ever brought home a treadmill and let it gather dust in the attic? Ever resolved on a diet, a course of yoga, a meditation practice? Have you ever felt a call to embark upon a spiritual practice, dedicate yourself to a humanitarian calling, commit your life to the service of others? Have you ever wanted to be a mother, a doctor, an advocate for the weak and helpless; to run for office, crusade for the planet, campaign for world peace or to preserve the environment? Late at night have you experienced a vision of the person you might become, the work you could accomplish, the realized being you were meant to be? Are you a writer who doesn't write, a painter who doesn't paint, an entrepreneur who never starts a venture? Then you know what Resistance is...

Have you heard this story: woman learns she has cancer, six months to live. Within days she quits her job, resumes the dream of writing Tex-Mex songs she gave up to raise a family (or starts studying Classical Greek, or moves to the inner city and devotes herself to tending babies with AIDS). Woman's friends think she's crazy; she herself has never been happier. There's a postscript. Woman's cancer goes into remission.

Is that what it takes? Do we have to stare death in the face to make us stand up and confront Resistance? Does Resistance have to cripple and disfigure our lives before we awake to its existence?

Resistance's Greatest Hits
The following is a list, in no particular order, of those activities which most commonly elicit resistance:

1. *The pursuit of any calling in writing, painting, music, film, dance, or any creative art, however marginal or unconventional.*

2. *The launching of any entrepreneurial venture or enterprise, for profit or otherwise.*

3. *Any **diet** or **health** regimen.*

4. *Any program of spiritual advancement.*

5. *Any activity whose aim is tighter abdominals.*

6. *Any course or program designed to overcome an unwholesome habit or addiction.*

7. *Education of every kind.*

8. *Any act of political, moral or ethical courage, including the decision to change for the better some unworthy pattern of thought or conduct in ourselves.*

9. *The undertaking of any enterprise or endeavor whose aim is to help others.*

10. *Any act which entails commitment of the heart: the decision to get married, to have a child, to weather a rocky patch in a relationship.*

11. *The taking of any principled stand in the face of potential reprisal.*

Resistance is a force you'll definitely encounter when trying to change anything that's difficult in life. As a matter of fact, it's likely the most prevalent obstacle you'll encounter. It would be nice if you could breeze right through life, but that's not reality. You're going to have to make some difficult decisions and make some sacrifices.

There are going to be days when you'd rather pick up some chicken nuggets and sit on the couch and watch TV instead of preparing a healthy meal and heading to the gym. Everyone has done this at some point, including myself.

From here on in, you'll have to climb mountains you never thought you could climb. You're going to stumble at times, but just keep climbing. If you allow resistance to get the best of you, failure is not only possible, it's likely.

By learning to recognize resistance when it asserts itself, you'll be able to conquer it in the end. Any time you feel that you're struggling or not making progress, don't let resistance get the best of you. And don't give up!

6

DECLUTTERING YOUR FINANCES:
The Ultimate Path to Freedom

Before we dive in, it would be helpful for you to examine the way you think about money and personal finances. Today, most people look at money as a way to gain power and influence and/or to purchase items. For politicians and big business it's primarily about greed and power; for the everyday consumer it's about filling the void of unhappiness with shiny objects. I'll be focusing on the thought process and influence of money as it relates to the average person in society today.

I'll say this with as much emphasis as I possibly can: If you're struggling financially, you must change your attitude about what money represents to you in order to find happiness and live the life you want to live. Here's what money should truly represent to you: FREEDOM! I know it does for me. Every penny I earn and save is based upon the premise that it will it give me more freedom to do the things, and live the life, I want.

OK, I might have gotten a little ahead of myself. I probably need to throw in what the word *freedom* means to me:

I define freedom as the ability to live the happiest and most rewarding life I can live, as long as it doesn't cause harm or intrude on others' ability to pursue their own freedom.

Pretty straightforward, right? It kind of runs along the same path as *treat others as you wish to be treated*. I think you can now see how I look at money differently than most Americans today. When you look at money this way, it almost automatically takes on an altruistic sense and path.

In today's world, money is the most complicated thing humans have created that can generate happiness or inflict misery. Because of this, it's critical that you understand and master the concept of money. It can be a double-edged sword when used incorrectly.

People often confuse having and pursuing more money as a form of out-of-control greed. I do, and don't, agree with this thought process. As I've pointed out, money equals freedom, so you must treat it as a very precious item that needs care and attention. When your primary focus is on earning more and more money, well beyond your aspirations of freedom and happiness, that's when it becomes a problem. Unfortunately, in today's world greed has overcome governments, companies, and yes, sometimes even the average Jane and John in society.

Here's a way to look at money as it relates to freedom: The more money you have, the more possible freedom you can obtain. The more freedom you have, the less money it takes to maintain that freedom. I know these might not make sense at first, but here's an example:

Let's say you owe $100,000 in student loan debt. You'll need to earn more money, beyond covering all your other expenses, to pay that debt off. That debt inhibits you from going on vacations, paying off other bills, etc.

In typical society today, you move up the job ladder to make more money to pay the debt off. After years of hard work, you pay off the debt. At this point, your monthly income hasn't gone up, but your debt load has gone down. You now require less money to live on because you've eliminated that debt, thus giving you more freedom to do the things you want to do. The more you do this, the less money it takes for you to live the life you want.

Here are some crucial facts to help you understand why and where we've lost our way when it comes to our personal finances and personal responsibility:

- In the last two decades our consumer debt has skyrocketed. From 2000 to 2017 consumer debt has doubled to $3.7 trillion, which is in the neighborhood of $11,000 for every person accounted for in the United States.

- A GoBankingRates survey in 2016, conducted as three Google Consumer Surveys, targeted three age groups—Millennials, Generation Xers, and Baby Boomers and Seniors—and found that one third of the people surveyed had $0 saved for retirement, and 23% had less than $10,000 saved for retirement. That means over 50% of Americans have less than $10,000 saved for retirement!

- Another GoBankingRates survey in 2016 found that 69% of Americans have less than $1,000 in savings.

- As of late 2018, the United States Government is over $21 trillion dollars in debt, almost four times what it was in 2000.

- According to a 2018 article in *Forbes Magazine*, Social Security is already paying out more than it takes in and is on pace to run out of money in 16 years.

The above statistics and facts absolutely scare me and they should scare you as well. It's pretty obvious that we have a severe spending and savings problem in this county, starting from the top down. I didn't include this information to put you into a state of panic or cause you to want to curl up in the corner mumbling incoherently; I firmly believe in recognizing the problem and putting together a solution with solid planning involved. Debt is killing us, plain and simple. The solution: Get out of debt, save money, and pursue ultimate freedom!

IDENTIFYING THE PROBLEM

If you're serious about decluttering your life and living more simply, you're going to have analyze your current financial obligations and determine how you can become debt free, or as close to it as possible. It's pretty straightforward: If you can't manage your finances in your current lifestyle, how are going to do it when pursuing *The Simple Life?* The answer is, you're not. Just like your health, you need to develop financial discipline if you're going to find happiness and truly be free.

I know the negative Neds and Nellies are going to fight tooth and nail rather than admit they have a problem in order to fix their finances. Just like any addict they're going to say, *I'm not like the rest of Americans. I'm healthy physically and financially. I don't need to change.* Well, the statistics don't lie, and if you're reading this book I would say with a high level of certainty that you're part of the population who needs to change their life and habits for the better.

The below will not be an A-to-Z solution for your finances, but it will include the big pieces to get you started. It would be impossible for me to cover every aspect of decluttering your life in one book, and honestly it would be overwhelming. My goal is to have you identify the most obvious problems and start working on them immediately.

The next book in *The Simple Life* series is going to be dedicated exclusively to obtaining financial freedom, so be on the lookout for that in the near future.

Listing Your Monthly Expenses

I've found this to be true time and time again: People who identify and document the problem they're trying to correct are far more successful than those who don't. If you think you can fix your financial problems without writing them down and using basic math, you're greatly mistaken. The only way for you to see where you are financially, and where you want to go, is to document and track your progress. No excuses—just do it!

When it comes to figuring out your financial lot in life, you first need to take a look at your monthly expenses as compared to your monthly income.

Here's an example (for a family of four) of how to comprise a list of monthly expenses:

Mortgage/rent: $1,000
Car loan #1: $500
Car loan #2: $350
Insurance (all house, renter's, auto, medical, etc.): $500
Student loans: $700
Groceries/eating out: $1,000
Clothes: $100
Utilities: $200

Credit cards: $500

Entertainment: $500

Total monthly expenses: $5,350

Total monthly income: $6,000

Leftover monthly income after expenses: $650

I think I was generous, as I've shown earlier that most Americans have less than $1,000 in savings and zero saved for retirement. Don't be one of those people!

Take out a sheet of paper and list **ALL** your monthly expenses, your total monthly income, and what's left of your monthly income after expenses.

DEVELOPING YOUR STRATEGY TO BECOME DEBT FREE

I don't just throw the "Captain Obvious" information at you, but help you come up with a solution. Now I'm no financial expert, but I'm debt free and have been for a long time. I also own an off-grid home on 40 acres of land, a truck, a travel trailer, additional land, savings to live on for a year without income ... you get the point. And I don't just say this from an analytical pie-in-the-sky perspective—I live everything I talk about and teach, 100 percent! Not to mention, I've consulted and mentored several people over the years on how to get out of and stay out of debt.

So where do you start when paying off your debt? I always recommend starting on smaller revolving debt, usually credit cards. Why? First, they tend to have the highest interest rates. Second, getting that first bill completely paid off has a huge psychological effect. It makes you gain confidence that you can tackle your debt, rather than rock in the corner sucking your thumb and saying you just can't do it.

If you have multiple credit cards, start with the one with the smallest balance and pay it off first. Yes, even if that means you only make the minimum payment on the other cards. This also means you need to stop using credit cards completely—**NOW**. It doesn't mean paying off the lowest balance while you're still charging those $5 lattes and cool shoes on other cards in the meantime.

Continue this until all your credit cards are paid off, moving from the lowest to the highest balance. The only time I recommend you deviate from this is when one of your credit cards has an interest rate far higher than the others. Still, pay the smallest balance off first to get your feet wet and develop some discipline, then move to the high-interest cards.

If you have the discipline, keeping one credit card that accumulates cash points is a good idea. I have a credit card that collects cash points and I use this extra money to transfer into a savings account. But here's the catch—I pay that credit card off completely every month before any interest can be accrued, so those cash points are like free money! I know very few people have this type of discipline, but if you can do it I highly recommend it.

Once your cards are all paid off, move to the second smallest revolving debt. For most, that will probably be student loans. Now you may say, *But, Gary, my car loan is the second largest one.* Yes, but usually the interest rate will be lower on that. Another important point is that items such as cars, boats, RVs and houses can be sold. I've yet to find a buyer for credit card and student loan debt, but if you do, definitely take them up on that offer! And if you think that will really happen, I have a unicorn that poops gold nuggets I want to sell you!

Once you have your credit cards and student loans paid off, you'll be ahead of almost every American today. That should motivate you to look at your other expenses and pay those off as well. The best part is that you'll now have more free income to pay off any remaining debts.

I'll tell you this: Once I became debt free, I found a new freedom I had never experienced before in my adult life. From the time I entered college until I paid off that last bill, I had been in debt. That's pretty astounding when you think about it: The system is designed to keep you in constant debt and continuously spending money you don't have. When you live debt free and within your means, it returns the power and freedom to you, thus taking control from the companies, and federal, state, and local governments that in most cases don't have your best interests in mind.

Once I had accomplished my goal of being debt free, it was funny how things in my life just kind of got better. I slept better, I had less stress, and I also had a lot more free time because I was spending my free time doing things I truly enjoyed instead of working more to pay off debt. In addition, you'll be surprised how much time you can save when you're not researching and buying things you not only can't afford, but don't need.

STOPPING IMPULSE PURCHASING— DO YOU REALLY NEED IT?

Next I'm going to give you a step-by-step approach to purchasing far more wisely than you have in the past, and to start purging all those unnecessary items that have been weighing you down, thus inhibiting you from fulfilling your dreams of financial freedom.

I go through a checklist every time I want to purchase an item and ask myself:

- Is it necessary?

- How will it improve or make my life easier?

- Do I need it right now?

- Can I afford it?

- Can I live without it?

- Will it just sit and take up space?

Straightforward and simple!

Here's a perfect example—I'm an avid mountain and road bike rider. You want to talk about being told you need every shiny item known to man to participate in an activity? Today you can easily spend $5,000 to $10,000 on a mountain or road bike. I've even met people who will purchase the new model of a bike they ride every year, losing thousands of dollars on a perfectly good used bike that's just as good as the new one.

On average, I purchase a new mountain bike every five to six years, and it's the previous year's model on sale, saving me a ton of money. My current road bike is 11 years old and still works just fine. The only time I replace my bikes is when they're worn out and fixing them up isn't worth it and/or there are numerous technological advancements on the newer bikes.

Throw in all the accessories that are pitched to you—fancy helmets, gloves, riding jerseys, shorts, shoes, lights, gizmos, gizmos and more gizmos! I've heard every sales pitch known to man from bike salesmen telling me I need the latest and greatest equipment, which has no bearing on the enjoyment or performance of riding my bikes.

I've also seen bike riders' garages packed full of old bikes, new bikes, several helmets, parts still in the packaging … you name the bike item, they have it. This is the classic display of ultimate consumerism and cluttering. The next time you're walking through your neighborhood, take a look at the status of people's garages. Most are packed to the rafters with useless accumulated junk, sometimes leaving no space to park a car inside.

My riding gear consists of padded bike shorts and the same workout clothing I wear at the gym. Yes, I do have a helmet, gloves, and riding shoes (for the road bike only; I use my hiking shoes for my mountain bike), all of which I've owned for several years. As a matter of fact, I still use a twenty-one-year-old Ironman watch and a fifteen-year-old Camelbak hydration backpack! They work just the same as the new ones, so why would I replace them?

The reason I give you the above example is not just to show you how I save money, but to demonstrate that by not purchasing unnecessary or redundant items, you ultimately need much less space!

(BONUS) GARY'S EASY SAVINGS TECHNIQUE

I would love to tell you how I came up with this savings technique, but I'm really not sure. I do remember I started doing it in college, and I've been doing it ever since. The concept is so simple and effective that anyone can do it.

When I first started it in college I didn't have a lot of free money, so the scale was much smaller than it is now. The rule I employed was that I couldn't pay for anything I wanted to buy with credit; I could only pay with cash. Whenever I bought groceries, gas, or anything else I just couldn't live without (that was the old me), any change I received in dollar bills and coins had to be put in a jug. Yep, if they gave me back ten one-dollar bills in change, it went into the jug, no exceptions. I would use this technique for a full year, then count all the money I had saved in the jug. I would use a portion of the saved money to do something I enjoyed, such as go on a trip or purchase something I really wanted. The remainder of the money had to go into my savings account.

I've been using this technique for almost thirty years now. I still save my change of one-, five- and ten-dollar bills (not always the tens, but at least a couple hundred dollars' worth a year) after every cash purchase. Obviously, things have changed a great deal since I first started, such as the arrival of ecommerce stores. Heck, the internet was brand new back then. But now I use the cash rewards on my credit card just like I used to use cash in the old days. I also still make most of my purchases in person, in traditional brick-and-mortar stores with cash. On average, I end up with a couple thousand dollars in that jug at the end of each year, and I've been doing it for so long that it's second nature. Basically, I'm saving without really feeling like I'm saving.

I've found this is a great technique to build up your six to twelve months of emergency living expenses. Yes, I advocate everyone should have an emergency fund for living expenses. To start, I recommend starting with a six-month goal, but I really feel you should have at least a year in emergency funds to live off when/ if things go bad. I'll delve more into emergency living funds in the next book.

7

DECLUTTERING YOUR SOCIAL CIRCLES: How to Avoid Unnecessary Life Drama

For some reason, we hairless apes love to jam our lives full of unnecessary stress and drama. What I find amazing about this is that most of it is self-generated and can be easily fixed. Remember, humans are social beings, but that certainly doesn't mean you should surround yourself with people who cause you harm or emotional distress.

Historically, we *had* to work together in small tribes in order to survive. A human alone in the world was far less likely to survive than when in a group. Not only could we look out for each other, but we could also share the workload, primarily in the forms of hunting, gathering, building/maintaining shelter and child rearing.

As society has progressed (and I use that term loosely), especially with the advent of the industrial revolution and the accumulation of personal property, we've started to move away from our tribal roots to a more individualistic lifestyle. We rely less upon others for social and survival support and have become more self-absorbed, resulting in more fleeting relationships that are shallower and less substantive. We can now go through an entire day encountering numerous strangers, sometimes in the hundreds if we're in a city, yet feel very alone. The result: We're seeing a spike in depression (resulting in a 400% increase in the use of antidepressants since 1988), poor health, anxiety, loneliness and an inability to connect with people on a deeper level. Simply, we're putting outside forces and influences over the inside primal forces that truly make us happy.

Many would be surprised to know that in the late 1900s, as factories were starting to be built, Native Americans were still living what we call a "primitive lifestyle," and numerous white men were joining Indian society rather than living in the new modern world. What's interesting is that the opposite was not happening for Native Americans; they were not leaving their primitive ways, joining modern society and moving to cities. In fact, it was unheard of during that time. I use this example to show you that instead of progressing in our social relationships, we seem to be going in the opposite direction. We're hard-wired to be social, to be in small groups who support us, and to have similar beliefs … it's just human nature.

WHAT'S A SOCIAL CIRCLE AND HOW DOES IT AFFECT YOUR LIFE?

A social circle is two or more people who interact with one another, share similar characteristics, and collectively have a sense of unity. Historically, our social circle was our tribe, but today we can have several social circles with different types of people, likes and characteristics. For example, you can have a social circle that you ride mountain bikes with on the weekends, which may never interact with your core friends that you have more intimate and deeper relationships with in another social circle. There's nothing wrong with having more than one social circle, in my opinion, or having several for that matter.

The problem begins—and it's very common today—when we surround ourselves with people who don't share our common values. In the end, this can cause us a great deal of harm emotionally, and drastically inhibit our personal growth and our ability to accomplish goals and find true happiness. And sadly, in most cases this is completely self-perpetuated. For some reason, many of us tend to drift into relationships that aren't healthy or don't give us a sense of real community. Then instead of fixing the issue, we spend a great deal of time and effort during our lives dealing with these toxic relationships. I mean, are you surprised that supposed "reality" shows that focus on dysfunctional relationships and families are so popular today? It's truly a sickness!

The best example I can think of where social circles can sabotage someone's goal of improving their life is in the area of health. I've witnessed this time and time again while working with clients. We all know that changing your health is difficult enough, but throw in a social circle that doesn't support you and is actually trying to sabotage your efforts, and success will become almost impossible.

When people surround themselves with like-minded people when changing their health, however, I've seen the success rate shoot through the roof. Not only short term, but long term. That's why I always encourage people who are first starting out trying to improve their health to join a gym. Not only is it a place where you can hire a personal trainer if you need additional help, but it's also a place where people have similar goals. I have friends to this day in my social circle that I initially met at the gym.

Surrounding Yourself with Positive and Influential People is Key

Study after study has shown that the ways you act, feel and progress in life are directly tied to the people you surround yourself with. If you have negative people who are not encouraging or supporting you in your life endeavors, the odds of you being unhappy and unfulfilled in life are greatly increased. I wish I had the magic answer or could outline the psychology of why we participate in this self-destructive behavior, but I don't. Some people, no matter how miserable they are, primarily due to the people they surround themselves with, will never make the change. Don't be that person.

I have a simple philosophy: I would rather be alone than be surrounded by negative people who will eventually bring me down. There are billions of people on this planet, so trust me, there's a positive and motivating tribe to belong to for everyone out there. But just like anything, it takes a little work and time.

So how do you find like-minded people to surround yourself with? Let's say you're looking to get into road biking and want someone to learn from and go riding with. There are groups listed all over the internet who have regular meetups and go biking together. Another great way to meet people with your interest is to go to the place where they hang out. Looking for people to mountain or road bike with? Go and hang out at the local bike shops. Interested in getting in better shape? Join a small gym with motivated people who have similar goals.

Here are some things to consider when looking to join or create a new social circle:

- **Look for like-minded people.** They should have similar interests and goals as you.

- **Seek out positive people.** Positive people keep you motivated, and their positive energy is infectious ... in a good way. Avoid negative Nellies and Neds—they're not fun to be around and will eventually drag you into their world of negativity.

- **Evaluate how much room you have in your life for new friends.** Some people spread themselves thin by belonging to too many social circles or having too many friends. Focus on a couple that you really enjoy and make you a better person.

- **Find people who inspire you to do better.** I like meeting people who are ahead of me in something I'm interested in. As an author, I especially like meeting people who are more successful than I am in the writing world, as it keeps me motivated and pushes me. If you consistently surround yourself with people who are not as good or experienced as you in something, it's extremely difficult to get better at that task.

Firing the People Who Are Bringing You Down

Now comes the hard part, and this is where most people struggle. In order to truly be happy and live a simpler life, you're going to have to shed the people who are a negative influence in your life. Many of us tend to avoid ending relationships that are causing us pain. I've learned the hard way, though, that you need to nip these negative relationships in the bud. It doesn't matter if it's a family member or a friend you've had for decades, a bad relationship or friendship is exactly that. We tend to give long-term friends and family members who negatively impact our lives way too much slack, but it would be better to treat them the same as if you decided to not be involved with someone you just met. Dragging out these toxic relationships with family members and long-term friends can be very, very harmful, so just get it done and move on.

You have to realize that not everyone is going to be a good match for you. If someone in your life makes you feel down about yourself, doesn't share any of your interests or values, or is someone that you just don't get along well with, it's perfectly fine to move on and forward. People change, and a great relationship today may not still be one five to ten years from now ... that's life.

SOCIAL MEDIA: IS IT REALLY SOCIAL?

Those of you who follow me know I'm not a big fan of social media. In fact, I feel it has done more harm to human interaction and the way we treat each other than anything in our history.

The (now) billionaires who created social media never had any intention of it being for the greater good—if they did, they wouldn't be billionaires. Yes, that's just my opinion, but it's grounded in some fact.

The primary goal of social media websites and platforms was, and still is, for one thing and one thing only: to collect personal data. What better way to gather your personal data than to have you put all your most intimate thoughts, shopping habits, likes and desires in one place? The best part is you give it to them absolutely for free—what a deal! And if you have a business, it gets even better! Not only are you collecting all that valuable customer marketing information for them, in the case of Facebook if you want to grow your following or just reach some of the audience you worked so hard for, you have to pay for post boosts. Throw in the advertising platforms and these supposed do-gooders are making a fortune.

This personal data is sold to a multitude of industries, including the federal government. The data is used in various ways, but primarily to have products marketed directly to you based upon the information collected. Another way it's used is to make their advertising platforms more powerful which generates more income. And all of this was done 100 percent against your will. Dump trucks of lawyers put together complicated service agreements in order to dupe you into giving up this information which makes people rich by marketing products to you 24/7! Have you ever wondered how those products you were looking at on another website suddenly appeared in your social media newsfeed or somewhere else on the page? Now you know.

Can social media be a way to go when trying to find like-minded people? Yes and no is my best answer. Do I know people who've met and made friends on social media? (as in real-life interaction, not just via the internet)? Yes, a couple and that's it. Have I ever done it myself? Nope. Do I recommend it? Nope. Here's why: As I've said earlier, we're social creatures, meaning we need face-to-face interaction, not some remote, filtered type that has nothing to do with how human relationships really work. But today a lot of people like the easiest way possible … and when it comes to relationships, social media is the easy way.

Since the beginning of social media, I've seen it cause ridiculous amounts of stress and strain in even the healthiest of relationships. Why? Because it's not social or personal, it's a proxy for people to act in a way they would never act otherwise. Simply, because there's no face-to-face interaction, it totally changes the rules of how we treat each other.

Here's a perfect example of what happens all the time on social media:

A not-so-tough guy loves trolling social media, creating all kinds of drama by telling random people they're stupid, or idiots, for not believing in what he believes. First of all, he doesn't know these people and they don't know him. So his thoughts and others' thoughts are going through some strange type of filter that the human brain has a hard time comprehending. Because of this, social media has brought about an entirely new level of behavior in which someone acts in an aggressive manner who would not usually act this way in person or face-to-face. Basically, they can act like an asshole without any real-life repercussions. People can also create fake accounts with aliases and play make-believe as much as they want with social media. That's not to say they can't do something similar in person, but it's much more difficult.

We have five primary senses: touch, smell, taste, hearing and sight. These are critical survival senses and are used in many different ways, including deciphering if someone is friend or foe. But social media only allows for two of these senses—hearing and sight—and in a very limited manner when compared to a person-to-person setting. In other words, when trying to find a social circle or new friends on social media, you never know what you're going to get. You're pretty much flying blind. Humans are greatly flawed creatures, so why add more risk when you don't have to? I think it's much better to meet people and get to know them in person, even for a first meeting, instead of hoping someone is being honest with you on the internet or on a social media website.

To truly declutter your relationships and social circles you need to be searching for, and wanting, long-term and supportive relationships. It's not about quantity, such as having 2,000-plus

Facebook friends, but quality. For most, having five to ten close friends is manageable—anything beyond that starts to become emotionally draining and makes it difficult to have enough time for everyone.

DECLUTTERING YOUR MIND:
Your Brain Is Not a Garbage Bin, So Stop Filling it with Trash

We're just beginning to understand the intricacies and power of the human brain. The primary component of the brain is the neuron or nerve cell, and it's estimated that we have somewhere in the neighborhood of 100 billion neurons in the human brain. The total amount of connections between neurons and synapses (these are the neuropathways in which information is transmitted and stored) has been estimated to be over 100 trillion. A neuron is an electrically active cell that processes and transmits information by electro-chemical signaling. Unlike other cells, neurons never divide, and neither do they die off to be replaced by new ones. By the same token, they usually can't be replaced after being lost, although there are a few exceptions. You may be starting to see the importance of your health as I outlined in the beginning of the book, as it relates to the functioning of your brain. Simply, poor health equals poor brain function.

At any given time, your brain is transmitting, organizing, and prioritizing huge amounts of information. We call this process reality or consciousness. We're not sure exactly how it works or what consciousness truly means, we just know we're here, and our brains determine this reality. One little hiccup in this system and things can go wrong—very, very wrong in some instances. We may recognize improper brain function in the form of anxiety, depression, poor decision-making, poor cognitive function and/or diagnosed mental disorders, such as schizophrenia or obsessive-compulsive behavior.

In short, the human brain is the most powerful information-processing mechanism that we know of today in the existing universe. It's the key to our existence in this world and determines our fate...are we happy, sad, satisfied, dissatisfied and much, much more that we're just discovering.

The most important aspect to realize is that all organisms have two primary functions:

1. Survival

2. Reproduction

Our brain is the most powerful tool we have for accomplishing these two tasks. It's primarily hard-wired for survival, and it prioritizes storage of crucial events and processes information for this main purpose. Have you ever wondered why you can't remember where your car keys are, even though you just laid them down somewhere ten minutes ago, but you remember with vivid detail the time you burned your hand on the stove when you were five years old? Simply, burning your hand was imprinted into your brain because it was categorized as an event important to your immediate and future survival. This is what we would term also as learning. Learning is a critical element of survival—that's why we're in a constant state of learning. Have you ever heard the saying "Once you stop learning you're dead?" It kind of makes sense now, in a very primal way.

With the above information, I find it amazing that we treat our brains today like the local dump. We just shovel all kinds of nonsense and useless information in them like they're a bottomless pit. Even though we know our brains are incredibly powerful, we also know they have limitations. Otherwise we would remember every event in our lives with great detail, and be able to recall this information at a moment's notice.

We don't understand why or how the brain has limitations on how much it can store or recall, but I would guess it's for good reason. We also know our brain prioritizes information—if it's important you'll more than likely remember the event; if it's not, bye bye! Here's another important fact: The brain never stops. Because of this, it's responsible for consuming 25% of the total energy our bodies use every day.

DECLUTTERING YOUR THOUGHTS— THE MIND IS A TERRIBLE THING TO WASTE

These days many people feel overwhelmed, bombarded by constant negative thoughts, trapped, stressed out, and just flat-out unhappy. *Gee, Gary, you just painted a pretty crappy picture!* But here's the thing: You can control your brain and change your life for the better. That's right, you're 100 percent in control of your thoughts, which directly affect your actions and most importantly your life. Once you realize this, and turn down the noise of what we're told is important in today's society, things start to become crystal clear. The bottom line: If you want to live a simpler life filled with the positive experiences and fulfillment, you're going to have to change the way you think, and the way you treat that lump of moldable goo on your shoulders.

Going forward, I'm going to present what I feel are the primary problems cluttering your brain and then give you actionable solutions.

Why Multi-tasking is Actually Slowing You Down

I've made the argument over the years, while doing interviews regarding primal health and living, that the human brain is designed to focus on one task at a time and then move to the next one. Think of it this way—we were hunter-gatherers not too long ago, and hunting was a primary source of getting adequate calories for survival. While chasing or stalking your prey, you would have laser focus on the task at hand; if not, you would probably not be a very successful hunter, which would mean the difference between life and death. You wouldn't be harvesting nuts, building a shelter, and then hunting all at the same time. If you lived this way, you would simply be dead because you wouldn't be able to perform these tasks with the proper focus to accomplish them.

MIT neuroscientist Earl Miller mirrors my above thoughts, and notes that our brains are "not wired to multitask well ... when people think they're multitasking, they're actually just switching from one task to another very rapidly. And every time they do, there's a cognitive cost."

Studies have found that multi-tasking causes three critical hormones to be released: *cortisol* (a stress hormone), *adrenaline* (the fight-or-flight hormone) and *dopamine* (the feel-good hormone). Achieving tasks releases a dose of dopamine, so jumping back and forth between small tasks gives you a sense of euphoria (a quick fix), even though in reality you're accomplishing very little. In short, you become an addict to these little dumps of dopamine, adrenaline and cortisol, basically making you a highly-wound, addicted stress bucket.

A great analogy is that instead of sitting down and eating a healthy nutritious meal, you're eating a piece of candy every ten minutes in order to keep that instant feel-good high going. Which do you think is better for your long-term health?

I have firsthand knowledge as an author of just how unproductive multi-tasking can be. Writing books isn't easy, and it's almost impossible if you don't focus and dedicate your time purely to writing ... well, at least *while* writing. If you ask most productive and successful authors how they do it, you'll surely be told that they dedicate uninterrupted time to writing, and usually have a very strict schedule for this purpose. There's no stopping to check social media, answer emails or make phone calls—their time is 100 percent dedicated to writing and finishing the next project or book. Have you ever met that aspiring author who's been writing their first book for the last five years and it's still not finished? Well, I have a pretty good idea of why it's not finished and probably never will be.

In order to quiet the noise and block out those shiny little dopamine brain highs, you need to learn how to prioritize tasks. Trust me, you'll be far less stressed out and productive than you've ever been. And here's the best part: You'll also have a great deal more free time to do the things you want to do!

Every morning, take a few minutes to figure out what tasks you must get done for the day and rank them in priority of importance. Checking your Facebook feed first thing in the morning is not a priority! Here's an example of my day, based upon single-tasking and ranking of importance:

- Upon waking, the first thing I do is check my email. All emails that are time-sensitive I respond to; the others are left for later in the day.

- Feed and walk my dog.

- If it's Monday, Wednesday or Friday, I then go to the gym for an hour or so of cardio and resistance training.

- Have my first meal of the day.

- Work on projects for business, or conduct any interviews I may have.

- Spend 2 to 3 hours on current writing projects.

- Check email again and respond to any critical emails, or ones that I didn't respond to in the morning.

- Wrap up the day and unplug.

Are you seeing how straightforward and single-task-at-a-time my day is? Obviously, things come up and you may have to change the order of importance, or add or delete a task.

I'll tell you, I gave up multi-tasking about a decade ago, and I've accomplished more than I ever thought would be possible. I now focus on the things that are truly important and require my attention, and block out the rest. I spend very little, if any, time on time-sucking distractions such as social media, clickbait news, random texting, or getting involved in other peoples' life dramas.

Some of you may also now see why I tell my followers that in order to contact me they must fill out the email form on my website. Filling out the form takes effort, not like social media where you can just say or ask something on a whim, expecting an instant response or answer. In addition, if you want updates from me, you must follow my blog or sign up for my newsletter. Doing this allows me to more easily prioritize and accomplish the critical tasks for my business, thus making me more productive and giving me more free time.

Information Overload

Today, we have access to more information than we've ever had in our existence. You would think that's a good thing, but it can feel like an 800-pound gorilla jumping up and down on our heads. As I discussed earlier, our primary function is survival. Anything outside this is just considered unimportant information taking up space. From the moment we open your eyes in the morning, we're literally bombarded with information, much of it completely unnecessary. Our brains process information as it comes in, so the more that comes in, the harder they have to work. Too much, and we begin to feel overwhelmed.

According to Daniel Levitin, McGill University psychology professor and author of *The Organized Mind: Thinking Straight in the Age of Information Overload*: "We've created more information in the last 10 years than in all of human history before that."

I'd like to give you an example of how things have changed, in the area of access to information, from when I was a kid growing up in the 70s to today. I remember the day my dad brought home our first, and only for that matter, set of Funk & Wagnalls encyclopedias. I'm pretty sure my sister and I were doing our goofy childhood happy dance as my dad opened the box. To give you an idea of how big of an event this was, and how important that encyclopedia set was in my life, I can still vividly recall first setting eyes on them, and I remember the smell of those books to this day. In short time we had every one of those encyclopedias spread from one end to the other of my sister's bedroom.

These were our one and only research tools, as we had no computers, internet, smart phones, or even CDs for that matter—we were still listening to good old vinyl records! For a kid, this was the mother lode of information all in one spot—and they even had pictures. We lived in the sticks, so other kids in our area would come over to use them for book reports, or we would just go through them page by page to keep ourselves entertained for hours on end. Oh, how times have changed!

Some may think, *You poor soul, Gary, your generation was so uninformed back then.* I would say the opposite: My sister and I learned a great deal of educational and interesting facts from those books, and most importantly we remembered a lot of those facts. Can you recall what you looked up on the internet just a couple of hours ago? Probably not, because you were more than likely checking social media, scrolling through newsfeeds, and reading a lot of other information that had nothing to do with your original search. And during that time, you were probably exposed to hundreds of ads.

During an hour or so on the internet, you're probably exposed to more information—most of it useless and unrelated to your original search—than I would have come across from perusing those encyclopedias for an entire day. The best part: There were definitely no ads for vaginal cream, or a prescription drug that will give me chronic diarrhea or blindness as a side effect, in those Funk and Wagnall's encyclopedias—just pure information and facts.

Below is a comparison list (not comprehensive, but an example) of the sources of information I had access to as a kid and what's available now, as I'm heading toward middle age:

Young and Bright-Eyed Gary

- Television (no cable, a whopping four channels)

- Radio (terrestrial only)

- Books, magazines, newspapers (print only)

- Oral communication

- Educational institutions (brick-and-mortar schools)

Some of the above could and did have advertising, but at a fraction of the rate of today. Can you recall some of those old commercials? I can: "He likes it! Hey, Mikey!" I threw that in for nostalgic reasons—forty years later, I still remember it.

A Little Slower and Crankier Gary

- Television (cable, internet-based, satellite, access to hundreds of channels)

- Radio (terrestrial, internet, satellite)

- Books, magazines, newspapers (internet, digital, print, audio)

- Oral communication (maybe, if you're lucky)

- Educational institutions (internet, digital, print, audio, video, brick-and-mortar)

- Internet (general)

- Websites

- Blogs

- Vlogs

- Social media (increasing all the time)

- Smartphone

- E-reader

- Desktop computer

- Laptop

- Notepad

- Smart watch

- Health tracker

Today we're mercilessly advertised to on these platforms and many, many more; buildings, buses, cars, even educational institutions look like they're sponsored by every Fortune 500 company in the country.

So we need to step back and re-analyze what's truly important to us, and decide on what's critical for us to not only survive but to thrive in this world.

I have a very simple philosophy: Keep it simple and focus on the things that matter. With all the information now available at our fingertips, it's easy to get distracted and stressed over things that have nothing to do with us. Why do I care that Kim Kardashian got another butt-enhancing procedure, or that another shady politician just got prosecuted, or in many cases escaped prosecution for crimes you and I would certainly go to prison for? The next thing you know, you're in the comments section, wasting time and getting spun up emotionally in something that has no bearing on your life.

There's so much competition for your attention—whether it be news, social media, or the marketing of products you don't need—and if you *don't* make a concerted effort to turn off a great deal of this noise, you'll live in a constant tornado of self-imposed, unessential information mayhem.

My Top 5 Ways of Dealing with Information Overload

1. Create a short, concise to-do list for yourself every day. But don't do it right before bed, as it may make you focus on things you want to get done and interrupt your ability to fall asleep.

2. Don't multi-task. Most multi-tasking is caused by shifting back and forth between things that are non-essential: e-mail, social media, texting … you get the point.

3. Get your news in a small ten-minute dose in the morning.

4. Take a break every couple of hours and clear your mind.

5. Exercise with no distractions. Focus on the task at hand and don't listen to current event podcasts or anything that's going to add unnecessary stress to your life. The point of exercise is to get/stay in shape and decompress.

WHY SLEEP IS CRITICAL FOR YOUR BRAIN AND HEALTH

So many of us go through the day feeling tired. It's no wonder: In the past 40 years, adult Americans have reduced the amount of time they sleep each night by two hours! A recent survey found that many people sleep less than six hours per night, yet most researchers agree that adults need seven to nine hours of nightly slumber.

Sleeping patterns appear to have some correlation to body weight—as sleep time decreases, average weight increases. In

1960, only one in nine adults was obese. In 2007, this statistic jumped to nearly one in three.

Sleep difficulties visit 75 percent of us at least a few nights per week. A short-lived bout of insomnia is generally nothing to worry about. However, chronic sleep deprivation is a bigger concern, since it can lead to weight gain, high blood pressure, lowered immunity and poor cognitive function.

Some Useful Sleep Facts

- **Learning and memory:** Sleep allows the brain to commit new information to memory through a process called memory consolidation. In studies, people who'd slept after learning a task did better on subsequent tests.

- **Metabolism and weight:** Chronic sleep deprivation may cause weight gain by affecting the way our bodies process and store carbohydrates, and by altering levels of hormones that affect appetite.

- **Safety:** Chronic fatigue can lead to daytime drowsiness and unintentional naps. Such episodes may cause falls and potentially deadly mishaps, such as medical errors or air traffic and road accidents.

- **Mood:** Sleep loss may result in irritability, impatience, an inability to concentrate and moodiness. Too little sleep can also leave you too tired to do the things you enjoy.

- **Cardiovascular health:** Serious sleep disorders have been linked to hypertension, increased levels of stress hormones, and irregular heart rhythms.

- **Disease:** Sleep deprivation alters immune function,

including the activity of "killer" immune cells (the "soldiers" of your immune system that seek out and destroy threatening viruses and bacteria that have "invaded" in your body). Good sleep habits may also help fight cancer.

I know with our busy schedules, families and other obligations, it's often difficult to get seven to nine hours of sleep per night. But sleep goes such a long way toward improving your health and body shape that I urge you to try, even if you can only add a little bit of time to your nightly rest.

Before industrialized society existed, our activity and sleep patterns were very in tune with the cycles of the sun and our natural environment. Because of this long history, when light stimulates your skin or eyes, *regardless of the source*, your brain and hormonal system think it's morning.

Circadian Rhythms

Your natural or *circadian* rhythm is the "internal body clock" that regulates the roughly 24-hour cycle of biological processes shared by animals and plants alike. If we were to follow our natural circadian rhythms, we would start winding down as the sun set and would be ready for sleep by around 10 pm. Most physical repairs occur while sleeping between 10 pm and 2 am. After 2 am, and until you wake up at sunlight, your body is more focused on psychogenic (mental) repair.

Understanding how your body reacts to light is critical, especially in a day and age when we watch TV or play with smartphones in brightly lit rooms well past when the sun has gone down. In response to this light, artificial or otherwise, your hormonal system releases the stress hormone cortisol. This is because your body considers light to be a form of electromagnetic stress, and cortisol readies your body for activity and the start of the day.

Cortisol levels peak between 6 am and 9 am, but at the end of the day when darkness falls your cortisol levels are greatly reduced. At the same time, melatonin (a sleep-regulating hormone) is released, as are growth and repair hormones. The take-home message? Use light to wake up, and dim the lights (including smartphone, computer, and TV screens) well before you want to fall asleep.

Studies have shown that people who have chaotic, irregular sleep schedules tend to release excessive amounts of cortisol throughout the day. If you're one of them, you may consequently suffer from fatigue of the adrenal glands (which are responsible for "fight-or-flight" responses). Adrenal gland fatigue causes additional storage of stomach fat, thus contributing to obesity.

Alternatively, some of you may be concerned about oversleeping. To ensure you rise at a consistent time every morning, leave your window blinds open. This allows natural sunlight to enter your room, stimulating the production of cortisol and gradually waking your body. This could be impractical, though, if you live in an urban setting where streetlights are on all night and can disturb the quality of your sleep.

Consistency in your sleep patterns will usually ensure that you naturally wake at the same time in the mornings, or you can purchase a clock that gently wakes you by simulating the gradual increase in light of sunrise. This is much more pleasant to wake to than a jarring alarm!

Simple Tips for a Good Night's Rest

1. Reduce or eliminate your exposure to bright lights, such as fluorescent lights, for at least two hours before you go to bed.

2. Go to sleep by 10:30 pm. This means you need to be in bed by 10 pm to allow enough time to wind down and fall asleep.

3. Don't consume any products or drinks containing sugar, caffeine or nicotine after 1 pm. This will allow your body sufficient time to eliminate most or all of these non-sleep-friendly stimulants before you snooze.

4. Get some exercise every day. However, try not to exercise too close to bedtime. I recommend completing your workout at least two hours before going to sleep.

5. Make sure you've finished your last meal of the day at least three hours before you retire. A light supper will be easier to digest and keep you more comfortable as you prepare for sleep.

6. Make sure your room is as dark as possible during the night, or wear a sleep mask if it's impossible to eliminate light from your bedroom.

7. To prevent sleep-disrupting bathroom visits, don't drink any liquids two hours before bedtime.

8. Try reading an inspirational book 30 to 45 minutes before bedtime (no detective novels, however!).

9. Follow your body's natural rhythms. I know my body won't go to sleep if it's not ready. If I force myself to try to sleep when I'm not yet tired, I just remain awake for longer than if I had stayed up until I was ready to fall asleep naturally.

10. Follow a regular sleep schedule. You should go to bed and wake up at the same time every day whenever possible. I aim to do this even on weekends and holidays, so I don't have to readjust my sleep cycle when the weekend or holiday is over. When I sleep on a consistent schedule, I have a noticeable boost in my everyday energy levels, and I experience fewer sleepless or restless nights.

A LITTLE MEDITATION EQUALS A LOT OF CLARITY

I've saved a little woo-woo and inner hippie for last. There's been a great deal discussed recently about the benefits of meditation, but many people perceive it as mumbo-jumbo, or something only for hardcore yogis or Buddhist monks. Nothing could be further from the truth! Here's a little secret: Meditation is free, and there are no ads—you can't beat that!

I could go into a long-winded description of all the aspects of meditation and its benefits, but the beautiful part is that I don't need to. Meditation has been around for thousands of years, and I'll tell you this from a decade of firsthand experience: It's extremely beneficial and is incredibly simple to integrate into your life. There are a ton of books, for those who want to dig deeper into the subject, but for most the information below is all you need to start.

My meditative process takes just a couple of minutes, one to two times a day, and here's my technique:

- I find a quiet place with no distractions. One of my favorites is outdoors at my off-grid property.

- I sit in a chair or on the ground—whatever feels most comfortable.

- I close my eyes.

- I take ten deep breaths through my nose and release through my mouth, then do ten more, breathing in through my mouth and out my nose.

- I try to keep it somewhat rhythmic and to focus only on my breathing.

I kid you not, that's it. Just that short amount of time focusing on my breathing helps to clear my mind. I can't really explain the feeling afterword—it's just calming and peaceful. Not only has it helped me on really stressful days, but I've noticed I'm much calmer and more even-tempered since I started meditating. And I have a very busy mind, so if I can do it anyone can.

DECLUTTERING YOUR HOUSE:
A Bigger House Filled with More Stuff Does Not Equal Happiness

Our homes have become ground zero for today's out-of-control consumerism. The average American home has increased in size from 1,560 square feet in 1974 to 2,426 square feet in 2017, according to the U.S. Census Bureau. That's nearly double the size of what it was a little more than 40 years ago. Now, you might be thinking, *But, Gary, our families have gotten bigger.* Nope. The average American family size is 2.54 people per household in 2018, down from 2.97 people per household in 1974. As a matter of fact, average household family size in the U.S. is at its smallest in modern history.

There are two main factors driving the above. First, the real estate market has told us we need to purchase the biggest house possible, and the banks are more than willing to finance it for most of us. The increasing size of our homes is not based on sane financial decision making, instead it's driven by aggressive marketing and misinformation. Second, as we accumulate more things because we're told they'll make us happier, we need more space in order to put them somewhere.

According to statistics, you're more than likely one of those people in a too-large house that's stuffed to the roof with useless crap. I should know, as I was one of them too. So what do we do about it? Now, I'm not saying run out and sell your house tomorrow. I would recommend you downsize if possible, but I also know a lot of people don't have the option of immediately selling their house. In my next book, *The Simple Life Guide To Financial Freedom*, I'll go into the math of why your house is more than likely putting you in the poor house ... OK, pun intended.

This book is about getting rid of clutter, so before you make a decision on whether or not you want to downsize your house, you need to get rid of the useless stuff cluttering it and your life.

When it comes to decluttering your house, I always tell people to start with the garage for two simple reasons:

1. Most people's garages are ground zero for storing useless crap.

2. It will serve as your staging area for the remainder of your stuff when you progress to the inside of your house.

Here's your decluttering item checklist:

• Have I used this item in the last year?

• Does it serve a useful purpose?

• Does it give me any enjoyment (and not just from looking at it)?

If you answer **NO** to these three questions, it's gone. And "maybe," "sort of," or "kinda" are not acceptable—you can only answer yes or no.

To get your feet wet, put together your top-ten list of items to start with. Not in your head, you need to take out a sheet of paper and write them down. As I said earlier, I've found that when people write things down they tend to have a much higher rate of succeeding. Put it on the refrigerator, if you need to, so you have to look at it every day. Then the only way that thing is going away is for you to complete the list. Yes, this is a little shaming, but some people need this motivation. How are you going to feel seeing it every day, and worse when your neighbors and friends see it and notice nothing's happening!

I think most of you will feel that this process is pretty straightforward and easy once you get started. The hard part is actually taking the first step.

Once you've identified the items you no longer want, how do you get rid of them?

- Yard sale

- Craigslist.com

- eBay.com

- Freecycle.org

- Pawn shop

- Donate

- Give them away to people you know

- Put them on the curb with a sign (free)

I've used all of the above with great success over the years, but the one that's surprised me the most is setting them on my front curb with a "free" sign. Almost never has an item lasted an entire day without someone taking it.

Once you identify your items to put "Operation Get Rid Of" into action, you have 24 hours. No procrastination as that's just another way to put it off—get it done now!

Repeat this until your garage is cleared out. The job is not done until you can park a car in it, or two or more, depending on your garage size. The amount of cars it was built for is the amount of cars that must fit.

Once you have your garage decluttered, you'll use it as a staging area for decluttering the remainder of your house. *But, Gary, you just told me I have to be able to park my cars in the garage.* Yep, that means you better hurry! A really good systematic way is to go through a room a week, then do closets and storage areas on the last weekend of the process.

Not only will getting rid of stuff help cleanse your mental well-being and allow you to follow the life you want, it also teaches you the discipline you'll need to live The Simple Life lifestyle.

Just because you go through the initial decluttering process doesn't mean you're done. Here's a good piece of advice, and something I do on a regular basis: Twice a year I go through another decluttering process—once for my RV and once for my off-grid house. Yep, collecting useless items can sneak up on you if you don't do this. Before you know it, you're right back where you started if you're not careful. The best part is that doing this doesn't take long if do it consistently. For me, it's mainly building supplies and tools that I needed for a certain part of my project but no longer need.

Another benefit to creating a systematic decluttering process is that you'll start to declutter more and more every time. Not only do I get rid of things that I may not have noticed I no longer needed short term, but I've fine tuned the declutter process further. Meaning I'm constantly having to identify items that, on the first pass I thought I needed and were important, but now realize they're not.

I now own the fewest items I've had since my early twenties, well before I owned my first house. And, surprisingly, I would argue that I'm the happiest I've ever been—financially secure, with more free time and a true sense of purpose. Those useless items I spent hours and hours researching, purchasing, then storing have no power over me now … because they're no longer around.

Your house is there for you to live and sleep in, and if purchased correctly is an investment—it's purpose is not to store useless items. If you're properly pursuing *The Simple Life*, you should be spending less and less time in your house, and much more time enjoying yourself outdoors and in other places that give you joy. That's not to say your house is a bad place, but it shouldn't be the main focus of your life.

In closing, I want to emphasize that the above doesn't mean you should only have a couple of lawn chairs in your living room and be making animal silhouettes on the wall with your one lamp. But some will go to this extreme and head toward a minimalist lifestyle, which is (by most minimalist's definition) living with 100 or fewer possessions. This movement has really taken off, especially with Millennials, and I wouldn't argue against if it's something you want to work toward. Remember, for most of our history we only owned things we could carry on our back.

10

DECLUTTERING YOUR TECHNOLOGY DEVICES: Do You Really Need That New Gadget?

Today's younger generation doesn't really know life without technology, such as smartphones, laptop computers, tablets, e-readers, smart watches, health monitors and much more. We older folks, myself included, grew up not only when none of the above existed, but when their existence was still far in the future.

To give some of you younger folks an example, when I was young I watched the evolution of music go from vinyl records, to eight track tapes (ask your mother or father what these were), to cassette tapes, to CDs, and eventually to digital downloads and the devices that go along with them. The younger generation knows music only in the digital format. Though it appears vinyl records are making a comeback, which is pretty cool for us old farts because they do sound better than their modern digital format.

To say the least, technology has progressed in leaps in bounds during my lifetime, primarily in the last ten years.

How many people do you know who own a desktop computer, laptop, tablet, smartphone, smart watch, health tracker, and even a smart TV? I'm not talking about just one or two of the above, but all of these devices if not more. I know several people who own all of these technology-based devices.

Modern technological devices represent a double-edged sword. In some cases these devices can make your life easier, but they can also cause feelings of anxiety, agitation, and even anger because you want to destroy them out of pure frustration. Just like those random useless possessions cluttering your house, technological devices, even though small in size, can have massive consequences in the form of mental clutter.

If you were to add up the time you spend on your technological devices on a daily basis, I bet it would far outweigh the time you spend in person-to-person interaction. I know some of you are saying you get a ton of person-to-person interaction—on social media, interactive video games, and Facetime—but that's not real human interaction. Remember all the filters I discussed earlier in this book when you rely primarily on this type of human interaction? Flat-out, it's not the same thing, and it's a very new and foreign way for humans to interact.

The average American now spends one third of their waking hours on their smartphone—a whopping 4.7 hours a day according to new findings from Informate Mobile Intelligence, a Seattle-based research group that tracks and measures consumer use. It gets worse:

According to a survey released by AT&T and the Center for Internet and Technology Addiction, 61 percent of Americans sleep with their phones and 53 percent get upset if they're without their phones. Not to mention, they also check social media an average of 17 times a day. There's actually a new physical condition called "text neck," which is neck pain and damage sustained from looking down at your cellphone, tablet, or other wireless device too frequently and for too long.

I've seen estimates that the average American spends close to ten hours a day on the technological devices I mentioned above. Remember, these devices have ridiculous amounts of storage capabilities. Unlike your home, where the clutter is in the form of physical objects, we're now talking about digital information clutter. Simply, the more devices you have, the more digital clutter you'll have. My smartphone alone has a data storage capacity that can hold more information than I could ever look at in my lifetime, many times over.

You have two primary areas of clutter when it comes to today's technological devices:

1. Having unnecessary technology devices you don't need

2. The terabytes of information stored on these devices that can clutter your brain

I run a business almost entirely built on modern technology, and I have a fraction of the devices the average American has. I run my business on three primary modern technology devices:

1. A laptop

2. A smartphone

3. A remote internet connection (a mobile wi-fi device)

Yep, that's it. I don't own any other technology devices. Heck, I would go back to a flip phone tomorrow if I didn't have to respond to work-based emails when away from home or on the road.

I'm pretty sure most Americans stuffing their lives with numerous devices don't run a business with them, but use them mostly to waste time, and are more unproductive as a result. Another aspect of these devices is that once you get sucked into their "buy-me" vortex, you're constantly replacing an old one with a new one—in a lot of cases once a year or so. That's thousands and thousands of dollars you more than likely don't really have, spent on items you don't really need.

How do you think Apple has more free cash than numerous countries' yearly Gross Domestic Product (GDP) in the world? By making you continually upgrade to that "must-have" product, because if you don't you're missing out! No, you're not. You're just blowing money and wasting time. Hey, I'm an Apple user, but I use their products as a tool, not as a shiny object I must have when a new product not much better than the last one comes out.

Not only are these devices causing you to spend money, but you also have to spend numerous hours learning all the functions of the newer version, or figure out a piece of unnecessary technology you're adding for no good reason.

I'm not saying you should go hurl all your all your devices into the ocean and completely unplug. What I am saying is that you need to determine which devices are going to make your life easier, and most importantly, which are essential. On average, I replace my smartphone every four years, and my laptop every three to four years, depending on wear and tear. I run my business on my laptop and I'm an author, so my laptop gets a lot of use. These two items are 100 percent essential for my business, and using them for anything else is a very small fraction of their total use.

Here's what I want you to do: Put together a list of all your technological devices and prioritize them in order of importance. And when I say importance, I'm not talking about "screw-off time," but something you actually need in your life. Then determine how much time you spend on all your devices every day. This will give you a clear picture of how you might need to re-prioritize their importance.

Then get rid of the devices that have no benefit in your life. If you don't have a business that uses these items and you have more than three, I would say you have a problem. If you own a business and have more than three, you should evaluate if there's an easier way to do what you do with fewer devices.

As an example, when I downsized from the cottage I was renting and moved into my travel trailer, I sold my desktop computer and bought a more powerful laptop so I didn't need both a desktop and laptop. Also, and this goes back to when I was using social media a lot more, I decided to have no social media applications on my smartphone. This pretty much guaranteed that I wouldn't waste time on social media using my phone when I didn't have access to my laptop.

Just like your house, make sure to go through your devices twice a year and remove any applications, photos, videos and documents that you no longer use. Have you ever seen that person who has about a hundred icons on their computer desktop? Don't be that person—it makes my head hurt just thinking about it.

I'll leave you with this one final note: Technology is great as long as you use it as a tool. I'm not saying to never use it for entertainment, but you have much more important things to do like exercise, spend time with family and friends, travel, and maybe even find that life purpose we talked about in the beginning of this book.

11

DECLUTTERING THE HOLIDAYS:
Are the Holidays About Family or About Selling You More Crap?

The timing couldn't be better for me to be writing this chapter, as Christmas is just a few weeks away. The holidays, instead of being a time of happiness and getting together with family, have turned into a ball of stress and an orgy of consumerism. Would it surprise you that most retailers make the bulk of their sales during the Christmas holiday season? Have you noticed that Black Friday, which used to be only on the day after Thanksgiving, now seems to last for weeks? Cyber Monday, Black Saturday, Black Sunday, Discount Dinner Shopping, Half Moon Blowout Specials ... you name it, it seems to go on forever. It even seems like every year the Christmas advertisements start earlier and earlier. Eventually we'll see ads for Christmas starting in January just to make sure you get an early jump on spending your money!

OK, you might think I'm an old bah humbug, but not really as I love the holidays. But I don't think showing love for my friends and family requires me to have money flying out of my butt at a disturbing rate.

It's no secret that consumer spending in the United States represents roughly 70 percent of our entire economy. Now there are all kinds of services included in this 70 percent, such as health care, groceries, vehicle maintenance, etc., but the bottom line is, we buy a lot of shit! It's estimated that Americans will spend over $700 billion during the 2018 holiday season, and around 15 to 20 percent of this money is spent online. Roughly, this comes out to $2,100 spent during the holidays for every person in this country . . . that's some serious cash! The funny thing is, that's the number for every breathing person in this country, and the last time I checked, 1-year-olds don't have credit cards or jobs. Well, maybe credit cards and a smartphone.

Considering that only 15 to 20 percent of holiday shopping is done online, that means 80 percent or more is done in the trenches—face-to-face in-store consumer combat! I don't know about you, but this doesn't sound like a fun, happy holiday season to me. Just search the internet for fights over Black Friday doorbusters—they're in the news every single year. Think about this: Our desire to buy a shiny object that we think is a great deal can lead to a fist fight with someone else who wants that same shiny object! That's total insanity to me.

You may be saying, *But, Gary, I do all my shopping online—easy peasy.* No fist fights or pulling hair to be had, just clickety, clickety, click. Well, yes and no. Remember when I discussed earlier how social media platforms are nothing but personal data-scraping software to be sold to the highest bidder? What do you think all those search engines and large online shopping retailers are doing? You guessed it, they're compiling all your shopping data to blitz you with ads until the day you die.

I know that's a little morbid, but I've been unsubscribing to retailers and companies I like for the last few weeks non-stop. As I'm writing this, it's two weeks before Christmas and some are sending me multiple emails a day—every friggin' day! I don't care how much I like your products, this is a sure way to really piss me off.

For people who are surprised that I don't run holiday promotions for my company, well, now they know why. I tend to run specials during random parts of the year that have nothing to do with the holidays, but more with giving my loyal customers a good deal from time to time. I know, a pretty crazy concept, disengaging from the monster marketing world we're told we (business owners) have to be a part of in order to sell products and be successful.

I know people who will wait all year until the Black Friday deals to do their shopping, not only for Christmas but also for personal shopping outside of the holidays. But here's a dirty little secret in the retail business that's really prevalent with the big retailers: Black Friday is a way for them to dump crappy products and get them out of their inventory. So that cheap flatscreen TV that you really don't need is more than likely a piece of junk that will have a very short life. Not to mention, the good doorbuster products are in very limited supply so you probably won't get any of them—they're just bait to get you in the door and possibly physically accosted. So the next time you're sleeping in your sleeping bag on the sidewalk or in line at 4 o'clock in the morning in your pajamas, just remember the above.

Wow, I know I've just painted a pretty ugly holiday shopping picture, but let me give you a personal story and share how I deal with holiday shopping chaos now. First, I grew up pretty poor, so our holiday shopping was never extravagant, and a good chunk of my presents were based on things I needed like clothes and shoes.

Fast forward to me being a poor college student the day before Christmas with a couple of my friends at a mall in Southern California. First, it took us about an hour in line on the freeway exit just to get to the parking garage. Then the fun began—the parking garage was a flat-out war zone. We saw fights over parking spots, two-car accidents, and just pure mayhem. We finally got inside the mall and it was wall-to-wall people, and not all of them were in the best of moods, me included.

After struggling to fight through crowds, and trying to sort through what was left of the products that my friends and family might actually like, I was mentally and physically exhausted. Not to mention, I didn't have a lot of money at this stage of life so all these gifts were purchased on credit. *Merry Christmas, Gary, you're now even poorer!*

I remember thinking, even back then, that the holidays just weren't a good experience with this out-of-control consumer model. So I came up with what I thought was a brilliant idea. The next year, instead of fighting the crowds and blowing a bunch of money I didn't have, I decided I would take my family out to dinner as an all-in-one Christmas present. My family is pretty small, though, so if you have a very large family this may not work for you.

The next year when I came home, I declared there would be no physical gifts from me. I told them to get together and pick a restaurant of their choice, and to choose any day before or even after Christmas. Once those decisions were made, dinner on me was my present to them. Yep, I got some blank stares and maybe even some whispering, "Gary is a lazy cheapskate." But let me tell you, we all had a good time at that first dinner, and a tradition was born.

For the last twenty-five or so years that's what I've been doing, and my family looks forward to it every year. Not only that, I've noticed that others in my family, and even some friends, have adopted my plan for other events that are usually gift-buying driven. Come on, everyone has to eat, and the last time I checked everyone likes tasty food so it's a win-win! Now I do zero thinking and stressing out about what gift so-and-so would like, or worrying if someone gets me a gift that cost more than what I spent on them. It used to just go on and on, but that's all over now.

I also told my friends and family prior to Christmas not to buy me any gifts, as I wasn't getting them anything. Yes, a very bold move on my part, but it had to be done. For the next couple of years they kept getting me gifts just like they did before, but they soon realized I was getting them nada—a big fat zero for Christmas in the form of physical gifts. My gift was spending some time together having a couple of beers, eating some delicious food, and enjoying ourselves. I didn't ruin relationships with any of my friends or family members and I don't remember any hard feeling at all for that matter—it was all positive after that first year.

It's just crazyland to me: We stress ourselves out and spend money most of us don't have. For what? Who wins during the holidays? The big stores, and companies that could care less whether or not you enjoy your Christmas. The holiday shopping season is based on one thing and one thing only ... to get you to spend money purchasing a bunch of things you and others don't need. It has absolutely nothing to do with happiness.

So now that I've made you want to crawl in a hole and bury yourself during the holidays, let's get to some solutions to beat the holiday stress, and stop you from digging yourself deeper into debt.

My Solutions and Alternatives to the Holiday Craziness

1. Instead of buying gifts, have a family dinner at a good restaurant.

2. Place a limit on who gifts are bought for (immediate family) and a price limit. (I would recommend $25 or less—that keeps it easy and more personal).

3. Make it a rule that everyone has to make their gifts by hand, no storebought gifts. That's truly a gift from the heart.

4. Do a gift exchange so every member buys one gift only, again with a price limit of $25 or less.

5. If the holidays are just too much, and you notice you get depressed every year, plan your vacation around this time and get out of Dodge.

6. Limit the holiday parties you attend—you don't need to go to every one you're invited to.

7. If you've decided I'm an idiot and I suck, and no way are you going stop buying gifts for everyone within a hundred-square-mile radius, at least use gift cards instead of wasting a bunch of time and effort that could be spent doing something much more productive.

Is it possible some feelings will get hurt if you implement a far less consumer-driven way of dealing with the holidays? Possibly, but if people get their feelings hurt from you trying to live a simpler, more happiness-based, less stuff-driven life, you might need to reevaluate those relationships as I outlined earlier in this book. Again, this is not about doing what society and other people think you should do. This is about you living the life you want, and doing it in a manner that fits within your goals.

Trust me, when I first starting writing this chapter I knew I was going to ruffle some feathers, but as those who follow me know, I'm not going to candy-coat anything. This was something that had to be said. And if you're taking it as some stance on religion, or anything outside of what it is (consumerism at its worst), you're completely missing the point.

Two primary aspects of our lives, money and time, are directly related to how we interact with the holiday season today. And the two main things people complain about not having enough of are money and time. Well, if you don't take a look at every piece of your life that's directly affecting the above two problems, you're not really in this to fix the things that are truly broken. To me, this is one of the easiest and most painless problems to deal with, but we've been programmed to believe that in order to enjoy the holidays, we must spend money at the speed of light which results in unnecessary stress and the opposite of happiness. It just doesn't make sense to me.

As a matter of fact, if I see another jewelry commercial during the holidays telling me the only way my significant other will ever truly love me is if I buy her literal shiny objects, I'm going to lose my mind. I won't even get into how that jewelry is mined with slave labor, and puts people in terrible and dangerous conditions, including the deaths of the people mining it in some cases. And the best part is that as soon as you buy that shiny object it loses over half its value, but don't worry about that, just keep buying!

12

Picking Sides: Keeping Us Pitted Against Each Other Means They're Winning and We're Losing!

It appears that I've saved the last two chapters to get everyone frothing at the mouth. I hope not, actually, as I'm trying to help you better deal with the primary things derailing your life and slowing you down, and I want to give you some sensible solutions that make sense. As those who've read my books and followed me over the years know, I don't put political opinions in my writings or skew anything based on political beliefs. When helping people, I think there's no place for political opinions or biases of any sort.

From time to time, people have tried to pigeonhole or categorize me into one political side or the other. Those people are so dug in on their political beliefs that they instantly try to classify me, or what I have to say, as something political. If you're one of them, please take this book, smack yourself in the head, and try again.

Here's the thing: This chapter will be the most political thing

I've ever written and, guess what, no politics will really be discussed. Huh? That's right, I'll be talking about politics from a tribal perspective, which is us picking sides and waging war on each other.

For those who may be unfamiliar with my background, by the time I left the federal government I had spent half of my life in it. So I don't say what I'm going to say from some theoretical bullshit perspective. I was there! I've stood next to some of the most powerful politicians in the world, on both sides of the aisle, including U.S. presidents, and heard their private conversations. And believe me, it opened my eyes to what politicians in this country really think of the people they supposedly represent (you and me).

What I've found the most surprising is that most Americans have no idea how our government works today—they just pick a side that they think aligns with their beliefs. In many cases, they're unsure of what those beliefs even are. I have a saying that I've used during interviews when discussing picking sides in politics:

How do you want your shit sandwich? Chunky or smooth?

When it comes to our political parties, I can guarantee you'll eat that shit sandwich one way or another. The goal of most politicians is to get you to eat as many of those shit sandwiches as you possibly can, while smiling with their hand out.

I find it baffling that most Americans fail to realize our elected officials work for us—we pay their salaries. OK, it can be argued that they're also paid by banks, special interest groups, and the corporate elite to get what they want: more power and money. Not only will I **not** argue against that point, I'll agree with it. But I want to discuss, not so much what the political parties are doing, and doing to us, but more of how they're keeping us at each others' throats, so they can keep on doing what they do ... spending our money like drunken sailors and enriching themselves and their buddies.

These days there's a term called *political tribalism*. Simply, this is picking one of the two main political parties (Democrat or Republican) and identifying with only that side's beliefs, thus making anyone belonging to the other side the enemy. I think you can instantly see the danger of political tribalism. By following this mindset, you shut yourself off from others' opinions which can manifest itself into an idealistic form of hate. This is not good, and the intention of this chapter is to try to stop and reevaluate this type of thinking. I believe this is incredibly important, as political tribalism is on the rise.

To give you an example of how dangerous political tribalism can be, below are the top mass-murdering political leaders in the history of our world who used political tribalism in one form or another to commit their human atrocities:

1. MAO ZEDONG *China (1949–1976)*
Regime: Communist **Victims:** 60 million

2. JOSEPH STALIN *Soviet Union (1929–1953)*
Regime: Communist **Victims:** 40 million

3. ADOLF HITLER *Germany (1933–1945)*
Regime: Nazi dictatorship **Victims:** 30 million

These top three mass-murdering political leaders are responsible for killing well over 100 million people. Let that sink in for a minute—you're now starting to see why I couldn't *not* include this chapter when discussing the things that are destroying our lives and making us miserable along the way. And again, for the most part it's self-imposed misery, as we can control what group we belong to (I would highly recommend not belonging to either) and how they influence us. I could have easily included 10 to 15 more examples, adding several million more dead to the total, but I think you get the idea. Simply, political tribalism kills ... literally.

Some may be saying, *OK, but that was a long time ago.* Umm, no. All three happened within the last 100 years!

When it comes to political affiliations and the strong beliefs that arise from them, I've seen numerous families torn apart, marriages ended, and friendships destroyed. Not to mention witnessing the nutjobs who go and kill innocent people because of their beliefs in a certain political party or ideology.

This has to end. We need to once again turn off the noise, as political disputes do nothing to improve our lives. In fact, they do the opposite—they cause pain and misery and are just a flat-out waste of time and effort. Ask yourself, how much time do you waste winding yourself up listening to political talk radio, watching the supposed "news," and jumping on social media to tell everyone how right your group is and how stupid and misinformed they are if they don't believe in the same thing? If you're one of the people who regularly does this, ask yourself, could your time be better spent? Is there a better way to not only effect change in your life but in the world in general? I would say absolutely yes.

Here's a simple fact: Both Democrats and Republicans are right, and at the same time wrong. I've found that statistics represent this by showing that most people consider themselves Independents.

In Pew Research Center surveys conducted in 2017, 37% of registered voters identified as Independents, 33% as Democrats and 26% as Republicans. When the partisan leanings of Independents are taken into account, 50%

*either identify as Democrats or lean Democratic, and
42% identify as Republicans or lean Republican.*

OK, read that last paragraph one more time. Today, even when people consider themselves Independent, most still show partisan leanings. I personally say screw both sides, but I also understand that people will have a leaning in some instances more toward Republican or Democrat. With that being said, I've found for myself that belonging to neither group feels much more sane, and my life is better for it. My belief system has many pieces, some of which could be considered leaning one way or the other, and I'm very often in the middle of the two.

WHY THEY WANT YOU TO PICK A SIDE

Politicians are smart and devious when it comes to remaining in power. By separating us and pitting us against each other, they have greater influence upon us and have a better chance of staying in office. Here's how (and both sides do this; it's not exclusive to either party): Whenever you put two people into two separate ideological groups, you limit their ability to gather and interpret information. How can you make a well-rounded and logical decision when all you're getting is one side of the story? By picking a side and digging in your heels, you've now closed yourself off from all, or most, information that doesn't align with your party's beliefs. Politicians know if they get you into their camp and close you off from the other side's arguments, you'll more than likely continue to vote for them, no matter what they do. "Sure, I embezzled, cheated, and was bribed, but look at what the (insert political party) did."

Both sides use sleight of hand to get you off the trail of what they're really doing. But here's the kicker, and this is from personal observations: Political foes act very differently on TV and in public than they do privately. On TV they will battle and call each other all kinds of names, but then you'll see them behind closed doors they're all buddies.

Have you ever noticed all the fireworks during senate hearings over some pretty serious allegations, yet nothing ever seems to happen? They're all in it together and they know if they really do something against a supposed political foe, they're going to upset the apple cart that they all benefit from. Simply, it's all theater—most of these members on the Senate Investigative Committee couldn't investigate themselves out of a paper bag. I was a criminal investigator and, trust me, there are no real investigators in the Senate. It's all for show.

They Belong to an Exclusive Millionaire's Club

Here are some alarming stats and facts to further prove my point:

- Almost half of the Senate and House members have been serving for over ten years. (I guess that public service is just too good to leave—there will never be term limits, trust me on this one).

- Members of Congress (2018) and their staffs owe about $10.5 million (U.S.) in unpaid taxes, one of the highest rates of tax non-payment of any part of the federal government, according to the Internal Revenue Service. In 1998, this same Congress made non-payment of taxes a firing offense for IRS workers. (Try not paying *your* taxes and see what happens).

- As of 2016, over three quarters of The Senate Judiciary Committee members were millionaires, and over half were multi-millionaires. The Senate Judiciary Committee is one of the most influential bodies in government, responsible for Department of Justice oversight, civil liberties legislation, and the vetting of Supreme Court nominees.

- In 2014, for the first time in history, more than half the members of Congress were millionaires, according to analysis of financial disclosure reports conducted by the non-partisan Center for Responsive Politics. Of the 534 members of the House and Senate in 2014, 268 had an average net worth of $1 million or more, up from 257 members in 2012. In 2011, the median net worth for members of the House and Senate was $1,008,767.

- Members of Congress become eligible to receive a pension at the age of 62 if they've completed a total of five years of service. Members who have completed a total of 20 years of service are eligible for a pension at age 50, or at any age after completing a total of 25 years of service. (Definitely not the same retirement system I was on while in the federal government).

- In 2011 Congress passed The Stock Act, making it illegal for them and their staffers to inside trade. It appears they were allowed to trade with insider information prior to this, though—sorry, Martha Stewart. In 2013, they quietly gutted the law, but said it was still illegal for them and anyone to inside trade with the sensitive information they're exposed to while in office (sure—wink, wink). There's currently no limit on the amount of non-salary income members can retain from their investments, corporate dividends, or profits while in office.

- Combined, the Senate and House of Representatives have a net worth of several billion dollars. Pretty amazing considering there are only 535 members total!

Hmm, I worked with and had interactions with probably over a thousand, if not many more government employees during my career, and I never met one millionaire in the bunch (except high-ranking bosses who were politicians with a job title). It appears this is an exclusive club for politicians. I could go on and on, but this is to show you that picking sides is absolutely pointless. Both sides are looking out for themselves, definitely not for you or me.

THE NEWS MEDIA IS STOKING THE FLAMES

It's my personal opinion that the news media died a long time ago, right around the time social media started to really take off. It no longer became about the news, but more about stirring the pot with clickbait and controversial headlines, which usually had nothing to do with the article or segment. The bullshit our news media now puts out, what most call "fake news," is the false and misleading information of the past, on steroids. Today it's almost impossible to find anything that resembles facts, or what I would consider professional reporting. Remember those investigative reporters back in the day, you know the ones who broke Watergate or the Monica Lewinski story? I haven't seen the title of investigative reporter on an individual in the media's bio or job description in a very long time. And if I do, I usually dig into their background to find they have nothing in there that would qualify them as a real investigative reporter.

Here's another key: The biggest news networks in this country are owned by massive corporations that are politically skewed and donate large sums of money to their preferred side's political campaigns. If you can't see that this is a huge conflict of interest and a problem, I think you know what you're supposed to with this book … Yep, smack yourself in the head with it and start again.

Today's news media is in bed with the politicians, so you're basically being given the information, and only the information, they want you to have. So, say you're a die-hard MSNBC or Fox News fan—guess what, you're only getting mostly one side of the story. I'm sorry, but that's not news, it's propaganda. Trust me, I'm a writer, and I do this crazy thing called research, which is becoming a lost art in my profession as well. It's getting harder and harder for me filter fact from fiction. Without my background as an investigator, I'm not sure I could even write anything that's based on fact … yes, it's that bad.

But, Gary, I get my news on social media, you might say. Again, you know what to do with this book. Every social media CEO and/or head of a social media company has a political slant that runs right into their social media platform—big time. I don't care which side they're on, that's bad for America, period! Are we surprised that the "outstanding citizen" (Mark Zuckerberg) who's been stealing all your personal information and selling it to everyone in the world—literally—has presidential aspirations? Oh boy, just imagine that shit sandwich as a double decker now!

Here are some alarming facts when it comes to good old social media and fake news:

1. 62 percent of US adults get news on social media (this is a serious problem).

2. The most popular fake news stories were more widely shared on Facebook than the most popular mainstream news stories.

3. Many people who see fake news stories report that they believe them.

It appears that we're not only wasting huge amounts of time on social media, but we're relying upon it to be informed on what's going on in the world. I really can't make this up—and we wonder why our lives are such a shit show!

THE SIMPLE SOLUTION: IT ONLY AFFECTS YOU IF YOU LET IT

OK, now that I've once again depressed everyone, here's a solution that not only allows you turn off the noise, but make and effect change in the positive.

It's pretty obvious to me, and I hope to you, that our federal government is a mess. I know you may think that it's hopeless, but it really isn't. Remember, they represent us, not the other way around. But picking a side, digging our heels in, and fighting each other is a road to nowhere. As a matter of fact, that's just what they want: to keep us divided.

Remember in the beginning of this book how I described how humans' success over millions of years has been greatly accredited to working together for a common goal? Well, we need to stop fighting each other with false, skewed information and focus on the problem: corrupt politicians who are only in the game for greed and power. We elect them, and no matter what party they belong to, we need to get rid of the bad ones and replace them with people who have our best interests in mind. Yes, it's a very difficult task, but it can be done. If we continue to vote blindly along political party lines alone, it's only going to get worse because we will never get the right people in office.

Changing the Things You Can Change—Now!

By keeping us divided, politicians and media also give us the illusion and belief that we're powerless. But this couldn't be further from the truth—we need to reconnect and realize we're free, and we make our own decisions. Instead of beating your head against the wall and getting all wound up by social media, talk radio, and the news, how about you ignore them and go do something about the things you believe in? Remember me talking about finding your purpose at the beginning of this book?

I've seen this firsthand, as I hang out with a lot of people and communities who have the same freedom-based beliefs I talk about in my books and on my website. Here's one of the biggest problems I see today: When it comes to people focusing their energies to fight for what they believe in, they're often actually doing the opposite. Again, this is part of their (politicians and big corporations) plan, to get you to waste your energy on things they want you to think are important. That way you can't get the things done that really matter. Here's an example of what I'm talking about below:

Ann is really passionate about climate change. She feels that we're greatly contributing to greenhouse gas emissions and she wants to change this. She's heard it discussed from one point of view only, and supports only the party that she believes shares her beliefs (little does she understand that propaganda shaped her beliefs, because she didn't do her own research.) She joins a group called The Climate Warriors (I made this up), and their main goal is to bring attention to their cause.

In order to bring attention to their cause, they decide to go to one of the Exxon Mobil buildings in a major metropolitan area. Their plan is to stop traffic on the freeway, at the exit that employees and managers at Exxon Mobil take to get to work. Another group will chain themselves to poles at the entrance, to make sure any workers who get past the first blockade can't enter the building. They've even decided to use physical force if necessary. I'm not making the above up—this is a plan that has been used by many, many causes, protest groups, and social justice warriors—or whatever they call themselves these days.

Their plan works perfectly: Traffic is backed up for miles on the freeway, no one can enter the building, and the news media is eating it up with a spoon. Sounds great, right? Then a couple of bad apples in The Climate Warriors have decided they're going to prove a point and "beat some asses," and now this event starts to become violent. Innocent people are harmed, some with possibly permanent disabling injuries, and numerous Climate Warriors are arrested. It's all over social media and the news, and they're spinning it to fit their agenda, even making facts up as they go along. This works out perfectly for them, as people are watching, clicking, and responding in the comments. It's an orgy of hate and discontent on all sides.

Now, what have The Climate Warriors accomplished? Absolutely nothing! They've pissed a lot of people off, done nothing for their cause, and managed to split the nation even further. The winners are the politicians, news media, and even Exxon Mobil, because in a lot of eyes they look like the victim.

I've found a lot of the people who use these tactics are not really that interested in the cause as much as they're interested in gaining attention for themselves. Now they have all these selfies, and more than likely videos, to share on social media, making them look like a hero to some. When in reality it's nothing but bullshit selfishness disguised as a cause. Are you one of these people? I hope not, but if you are, you need to really take a deep look in the mirror and figure out what your real life purpose is.

If this has pissed you off and you've thrown down this book, please donate it or give it to someone who's truly interested in not only changing their life for the positive, but in humanity as well. Again, I don't write this for myself, this is to help people. But I also know you have to *want* to change; I can't do it for you.

Let's say you really are truly passionate about your cause, not a poseur, as outlined above. Below is another scenario on how you can effect change and make a difference. Going after the big dog never works out well, as we can see. They have all the resources and power, and that's really difficult to overcome. Especially when you use misguided tactics. Remember that saying about how you eat an elephant? One bite at a time.

In order to do your part in combating climate change, you decide to move closer to your job so you can either walk or ride your bike. Maybe you even sell your car and rely on public transportation—all great solutions. Next, you decide to install solar panels, water-saving faucets and toilets, and LED lighting technology in your home. If you rent, you can still use many methods to reduce your carbon footprint—I've done it myself.

Next, you decide to organize a group and teach them how to do the things you've done. You and your group start going to city council meetings, sharing your story and indicating that you're interested in helping the town/city to utilize the alternative energy systems available. As a matter of fact, you and your group have already done all the legwork and found companies to provide the alternative energy products to the town/city, and it's at a discount.

You and your group take it a step further and create your own alternative energy company that provides products and services to consumers and companies in your area. Heck, you even find a couple of engineers who are interested in creating and patenting even better future alternative energy products.

But, Gary, you already told us politicians are corrupt. How will we do this? Here's the thing: It's much easier to effect change at the micro level than the macro level. Say you get no response from your local politicians, and the city council members refuse to let you participate in their meetings. You simply vote their asses out! You go door-to-door in your community and you let people know what their representatives are doing. You never know, one day you might be the one running for office to make sure your community's voice is heard.

You see the differences in the above examples? One creates discontent, anger and violence and changes nothing. The other puts positive action into practice, one step at a time, piece by piece. Posting the protest you were at on social media and arguing with people are not effecting positive change for you or your cause. What do you think is really going to make a difference—the shock-and-awe way or the flying-under-the-radar tactic? Using the second example not only gets things done, but doesn't shine a spotlight on you, thus those greedy politicians won't know what hit them.

I don't use this as some unicorn-in-the-sky type of example that will never work in real life. It's a fact that the second example I gave has already worked in towns and cities across the country.

Oh boy, that got a little long-winded, but this is incredibly important, as one of the major things causing people to be depressed and angry today is the discontent with our political system. By joining in the hate and following blindly, you're actually self-perpetuating your pain. By disengaging and focusing on what's important to you, your family, and your community—again micro to macro—you can help reduce that angst greatly and move your life in a positive direction. Simply control the things you can control and ignore the things you can't.

Trust me, I've been there. When I first left the government I spent a great deal of time reading the news and listening to political talk radio for a large part of every day. The result? I was angry, depressed, not so nice to be around, and all I wanted to do was talk about problems, never real solutions or focusing on the things that were important for me to feel fulfilled and happy in life.

We have to learn anew how to communicate with each other, and how to understand and listen to others' points of view. Not online or in social media, but in person. We need to be engaged, always trying to be better people, learning, adapting and most importantly overcoming obstacles in our lives without lashing out at others.

MY TOP 10 WAYS OF DEALING WITH TODAY'S POLITICAL AND NEWS MEDIA DISCOURSE

1. Get your news in small doses (10 minutes or less a day) and from multiple sources.

2. Don't affiliate yourself with one political party; take all political parties' beliefs into account and vote for the best candidates.

3. Don't be a political news junkie (see #1 above).

4. Go back to the old ways—don't discuss politics or religion at the dinner table or family events.

5. Instead of reacting, take action on the things you believe in.

6. Don't get your news from social media sources.

7. Don't engage in or initiate political conversations on social media.

8. Stay away from people who are always trying to engage you in negative topics you have no control over.

9. Focus on the micro issues affecting you in your community.

10. Don't donate to political parties (they will email and call you to death asking for more), only candidates or causes you believe in.

13

Finding and Dedicating Yourself to Productive Hobbies

Today I see two main problems when it comes to people being productive with their free time:

1. Our amount of free time is becoming less and less (this book is meant to help fix that).

2. We don't understand how to spend that free time, when we have it, to make our lives better.

We already have enough noise in our lives, and our free time is incredibly important, so why would we fill it with being unproductive or letting in more noise? I think for many today it's to numb ourselves and forget about the daily stresses we deal with. I know I personally struggled with filling my time once I decluttered my life and eliminated unproductive financial and time-sucking activities, such as shopping for shiny objects I didn't need, and watching political, divisive news programs. I was surprised by how many hours a day I spent on unproductive tasks.

I would say the big four time wasters for most are social media, watching TV, playing video games, and shopping (for unnecessary items). By eliminating or greatly reducing those activities, you can easily free up three to four hours a day. Surprisingly, as I found out myself, it was more difficult than I realized to fill those hours with not only something I enjoyed but that was also productive.

I'm one of those people who's easily bored, so too much free time by myself with only my thoughts can be a bad thing. I'm not saying that every waking moment has to be filled with productivity, but you need to prioritize your time and life. No more bitching about not having enough money or time—do something about it! Would it be better to play video games for a couple of hours, or work on that book you've always wanted to write? Would it be better to volunteer at an animal shelter for half the day, or shop for a new pair of shoes you don't need?

Decluttering your life is an amazing process. You'll not only find you have way more time than you had before, but you'll find you can add even more free time as you declutter more and more. Pretty cool, isn't it; the better at decluttering you get, the more free time you have. If that isn't motivating, I don't know what is.

I know if I hadn't decluttered my life, there's no way I could be the author I am today. Writing takes time and the ability to organize thoughts; decluttering allows me have and do both. Below are some basic productive hobbies I recommend to fill your new-found free time with.

1. Spending quality in-person time with family and friends.

2. Physical activity/exercise (you should have seen this one coming).

3. Cooking your own meals (it's hard to be healthy if you're not preparing your own meals).

4. Spending time outdoors.

5. Mindfulness (focusing on the moment and ignoring things you can't change or that are in the past).

6. Learning new things (remember what I said at the beginning of this book—if you aren't learning, you're dead).

7. Becoming more organized (I've found people who are organized tend to be more productive in general).

8. Volunteering or being involved in causes you believe in.

9. Reading (this goes along with learning, but not always. Those thriller and romance novels are a great way to disengage for a bit).

10. Becoming more self-reliant (those evil politicians don't like people to be self-reliant and do things for themselves).

FINAL THOUGHTS

To date, I'll say this has been the most difficult and most rewarding book I've written. In this book I was able to share my thoughts and experiences about how to live The Simple Life from a more well-rounded perspective. I definitely covered some touchy subject matter, but it had to be done, as people tend to shy away from these topics in most books. I didn't do it for shock and awe or to get people riled up, but from the perspective that these are critical problems we all face on a daily basis.

I'll continue to beat the "get healthy first" drum until the day I die. I've spent decades in the health, exercise, food, and drug industries, so this is from a deep perspective that most in this country don't have. I've seen it firsthand when working with clients: When they get their health in order, suddenly their eyes are brighter, they have more energy, and they tend to get their shit together. Your health has such a strong correlation and relationship to your cognitive function and better decision making, but you'll never know until you make the change. Again, I've seen it firsthand and also in my own life. I'm far more productive than I was in my 20s, which is pretty shocking.

We also know that having access to massive amounts of information today is a double-edged sword. First, there's no way you can ever find or use even a tiny, tiny fraction of all that information. Second, how do you decipher the good from the bad when there's so much of it? Our brains are being overwhelmed, scattering us, making our lives harder instead of easier. Throw in social media and non-stop marketing to feed the mass-consumer beast, and we're in very uncharted waters as humans.

The answer is to take a step back, reevaluate our lives, and figure out what's truly important and what will make us feel more fulfilled and happy. Is buying that 70-inch TV on Black Friday, or getting 100-plus likes on a post about our cat on Facebook, the answer? When I take that last breath and move on to my next journey, will I say "Damn right, I win, you lose," because I have more stuff and more followers on social media than you?

My goal, as with all of my books, is to give you something you can take away and use to change your life for the positive. Even if you disagree with me, maybe even at a high level, I at least want to get you thinking more openly about the topics I cover.

Divisiveness and hate are tearing this country apart, and all I'm trying to do is my part to get people to work together instead of drawing our metaphorical lines in the sand. If we continue to say, *You have to belong to such and such a team or you're wrong because you don't believe in what I believe in*, we're doomed. We need to analyze the facts from all sides and come to our own decisions, which in most cases are somewhere in the middle of all the noise.

I truly hope you find your purpose and passion in life, and just maybe this book helped a bit. That's all I can ask. I don't do this for fame and money, but to put a pinch of my ingredients into the positive-change pie.

For those of you who'd like to share your story of positive change, I'd love to hear about it. I still answer all my emails, which is getting harder, but I have it easier than most because my followers are out there making it happen and not emailing me pictures of their cat ☺. If you're subscribed to my newsletter you can just respond to any new update email, or sign up for my newsletter at www.thesimplelifenow.com/newsletter.

Finally, I want to thank all of you for making this possible. Without you reading my books, and the continued loyalty of my followers, I wouldn't be able to pursue my life purpose which I consider myself very lucky to be able to do.

Now get out there and make it happen!

Did You Enjoy This Book? You Can Make a Big Difference and Spread the Word!

Reviews are the most powerful tool I have to bring attention to *The Simple Life*. I'm an independently published author and yes, I do a lot of this work myself. This helps me make sure the information I provide is straight from the heart and comes from my experiences without some publishing company dictating what sells. You, the readers, are my muscle and marketing machine.

You are a committed group and a loyal bunch of fans!

I truly love my fans and the passion they have for my writing and products. Simply put, your reviews help bring more fans to my books and attention to what I'm trying to teach.

If you liked this book, or any of my others for that matter, I would be very grateful if you would spend a couple of minutes and leave a review on Amazon. Doesn't have to be long, just something conveying your thoughts.

Thank you!
Gary Collins

ABOUT GARY

Gary Collins, MS, has a very interesting and unique background that includes military intelligence. He's a former special agent for the U.S. State Department Diplomatic Security Service, the U.S. Department of Health and Human Services, and the U.S. Food and Drug Administration. Collins' background and expert knowledge bring a much needed perspective to today's areas of simple living, health, nutrition, entrepreneurship, self-help and self-reliance. He holds an AS degree in Exercise Science, a BS in Criminal Justice, and an MS in Forensic Science.

Gary was raised in the high desert at the basin of the Sierra Nevada mountain range in a rural part of California. He now lives off the grid part of the year in a remote area of NE Washington state, and spends the other part of year exploring in his travel trailer with his trusty black Lab Barney.

He considers himself lucky to have grown up in a very small town and has enjoyed experiencing fishing, hunting, and anything outdoors from a very young age. He has been involved in organized sports, nutrition, and fitness for almost four decades. He is also an active follower and teacher of what he calls "life simplification." He often says:

"Today we're bombarded by too much stress, not enough time for personal fulfillment, and a failure to take care of our health… there has to be a better way!"

In addition to being a bestselling author, Gary has taught at the university college level, consulted and trained college-level athletes, and been interviewed for his expertise on various subjects by *CBS Sports*, *Coast to Coast AM*, *The RT Network*, and *FOX News*, to name a few.

His website www.thesimplelifenow.com, and *The Simple Life* book series (his total lifestyle reboot), blow the lid off of conventional life and wellness expectations, and are considered essential for every person seeking a simpler and happier life.

Other Books by Gary Collins

The Simple Life Guide to RV Living:
The Road to Freedom and the Mobile Lifestyle Revolution

The Simple Life Guide To Optimal Health:
How to Get Healthy, Lose Weight, Reverse Disease
and Feel Better Than Ever

The Beginners Guide To Living Off The Grid:
The DIY Workbook for Living the Life You Want

Living Off The Grid: What to Expect While Living the
Life of Ultimate Freedom and Tranquility

Going Off The Grid: The How-To Book of
Simple Living and Happiness

REFERENCES

"1 in 3 Americans Have $0 Saved for Retirement." November 28, 2018. https://www.gobankingrates.com/retirement/planning/1-3-americans-0-saved-retirement/.

"2017 Report Cards: All Representatives." December 15, 2018. https://www.govtrack.us/congress/members/report-cards/2017/house.

"69% of Americans Have Less Than $1,000 in Savings." November 27, 2018. https://www.gobankingrates.com/saving-money/savings-advice/data-americans-savings/.

"A Deep Dive Into Party Affiliation." December, 15, 2018. http://www.people-press.org/2015/04/07/a-deep-dive-into-party-affiliation/.

"A Modern Spine Ailment: Text Neck." December 8, 2018. https://www.spine-health.com/blog/modern-spine-ailment-text-neck.

"Antidepressant Use Among Persons Aged 12 and Over: United States, 2011–2014, CDC National Center For Health Statistics." December 20, 2108. https://www.cdc.gov/nchs/products/databriefs/db283.htm.

Boehm, Christopher. *Moral Origins: The Evolution of Virtue, Altruism, and Shame.* New York: Basic Books, 2012.

Bowles, Samuel, and Herbert Gintis. *A Cooperative Species: Human Reciprocity and Its Evolution.* Princeton, NJ: Princeton University Press, 2011.

Calloway, Colin G., "Neither White nor Red: White Renegades on the American Frontier." *Western Historical Quarterly,* January 1986.

"CDC Smoking & Tobacco Use, Economic Trends In Tobacco." November 4, 2018. https://www.cdc.gov/tobacco/data_statistics/ fact_sheets/economics/econ_facts/index.htm.

"CDC Overweight & Obesity, Defining Overweight And Obesity." October 23, 2018. https://www.cdc.gov/obesity/adult/defining.html.

"Characteristics Of New Housing, U.S. Census Bureau." December 8, 2018. https://www.census.gov/construction/chars/completed.html.

CIA Library, World Fact Book. https://www.cia.gov/library/ publications/the-world-factbook/geos/us.html.

"Congress Is Now Mostly A Millionaires' Club." December 15, 2018. http://time.com/373/congress-is-now-mostly-a-millionaires-club/.

"Congress Votes To Eliminate Key Requirement Of Insider Trader Law." December 20, 2018. http://politicalticker.blogs.cnn.com/2013/04/12/ congress-votes-to-eliminate-key-requirement-of-insider-trading-law/.

"Congressmen Owe Millions In Back Taxes." December 13, 2018. https://www.theglobeandmail.com/news/world/ congressmen-owe-millions-in-back-taxes/article25459049/.

"Consumer Expenditures, 2017 United States Bureau Of Labor Statistics." December 11, 2018. https://www.bls.gov/news.release/ cesan.nr0.htm.

Geoffrey L. Cohen, "Party over Policy: The Dominating Impact of Group Influence on Political Beliefs," Journal of Personality and Social Psychology 85 (2003): 808–22.

"Hello? Americans now spend five hours a day—on their phones." December 8, 2018. https://www.washingtontimes.com/news/2015/ feb/10/smart-phone-nation-americans-now-spend-five-hours-/.

"Historical Debt Outstanding, Annual 2000–2018." November 27, 2018. https://www.treasurydirect.gov/govt/reports/pd/histdebt/histdebt_ histo5.htm/.

"Historical Household Tables, U.S. Census Bureau." December 8, 2018. https://www.census.gov/data/tables/time-series/demo/families/ households.html.

"It Can Wait Compulsion Survey." December 8, 2018. https://about.att. com/content/dam/snrdocs/It%20Can%20Wait%20Compulsion%20 Survey%20Key%20Findings_9%207%2014.pdf.

Lee, Richard (1979). "The !Kung San Men, Women, and Work in a Foraging Society." Cambridge.

References

"List Of Dictatorships By Death Toll—The Top 10 Biggest Mass Killings In History." December 15, 2018. https://about-history.com/list-of-dictatorships-by-death-toll-the-top-10-biggest-killers-in-history/.

"Majority In Congress Are Millionaires." December 24, 2018. https://www.npr.org/sections/itsallpolitics/2014/01/10/261398205/majority-in-congress-are-millionaires.

"Net Worth Of United States Senators And Representatives." December 18, 2018. https://ballotpedia.org/Net_worth_of_United_States_Senators_and_Representatives.

"News Use Across Social Media Platforms 2016, Pew Research Center." December 15, 2018. http://www.journalism.org/2016/05/26/news-use-across-social-media-platforms-2016.

"ersonal Wealth In The Senate Judiciary Committee." December 18, 2018. https://www.opensecrets.org/news/2018/10/personal-wealth-senate-judiciary-committee/.

"Political Typology 2017, Pew Research Center. December 13, 2018. http://www.people-press.org/dataset/political-typology-2017/.

"Report: Americans plan to spend nearly $720 billion this holiday season. December 11, 2018. https://www.ajc.com/news/national/report-americans-plan-spend-nearly-720-billion-this-holiday-season/fi76G7ezgnYE7jUOnfwoAL/.

"Sick Of Political Parties, Unaffiliated Voters Are Changing Politics." December 12, 2018. https://www.npr.org/2016/02/28/467961962/sick-of-political-parties-unaffiliated-voters-are-changing-politics.

Silverman, Craig and Jeremy Singer-Vine, "Most Americans Who See Fake News Believe It, New Survey Says." 2016. BuzzFeed News.

"Tribalism In Politics," *Psychology Today.* December 13, 2018. https://www.psychologytoday.com/us/blog/bias-fundamentals/201806/tribalism-in-politics.

"Trustees Report That Social Security Benefits Are At Risk In 16 Years." November 27, 2018. https://www.forbes.com/sites/kellyphillipserb/2018/06/05/trustees-predict-that-social-security-will-be-insolvent-in-16-years/#61f287be6120/.

"Majority of Americans Will Blow at Least One Paycheck on the Holidays," December 11, 2018. https://www.gobankingrates.com/saving-money/holiday/majority-americans-blow-least-one-paycheck-holidays/.

"More than $11,000 per person based on the $3.7 trillion debt divided by US population of around 325 million." Board of Governors of the Federal Reserve System, "Consumer Credit-G19." November 27, 2018. http://www.federalreserve.gov/releases/G19/Current/.

"Multi-tasking Is Killing Your Brain." December 4, 2018. https://www.inc.com/larry-kim/why-multi-tasking-is-killing-your-brain.html.